THE MC COOKBOOK

ENDEAVORS, STRUGGLES AND COOKING TRADITIONS OF THE MORMON PIONEERS

The Mormon Trail Cookbook is a historical collection of 367 recipes and remedies, some dating back years before the inception of the Mormon Trail. Many recipes were included in the book for their historical value and were not meant to be prepared; however, modern-day versions of some of these recipes are also included for your cooking pleasure. Enjoy exploring this collection of Mormon Trail history and recipes gathered from historical documents and the recipe boxes of modern-day cooks.

Additional copies of The Mormon Trail Cookbook may be obtained by sending a check for $10.95 plus $2.00 for shipping/handling to Morris Publishing at the address below. Order blanks are included in the back of this book.

Retail outlets may obtain The Mormon Trail Cookbook at special rates. Write or call to the address below for more information.

Editors: Dawn Feely, Cathy Foster,
Tamara Omtvedt & Shawnna Silvius
Publisher: Scott Morris

ISBN 1-57502-476-4

Printed in the United States of America by:
Morris Publishing
3212 E. Hwy 30
Kearney, NE 68847
(308) 236-7888

TABLE OF CONTENTS

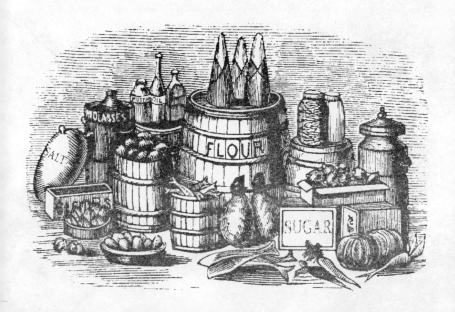

ABOUT THE ARTISTS

LYNN FAUSETT
1894-1977

The cover features a painting by renowned mural artist, Lynn Fausett.

Fausett was the born in Price, Utah, just 15 years after the first white settlers arrived. He studied art at Brigham Young University, the University of Utah and the Art Students League of New York, serving as president of the Art Students League for 14 years. He also studied abroad in France, Germany and Italy.

Throughout his career, Fausett painted many murals, including several for the Church of Jesus Christ of Latter-Day Saints. Fausett's work displays historical subjects and impressions from his childhood, including military life, ranch scenes, cattle drives and Utah canyon country.

WILLIAM HENRY JACKSON
1843-1942

The paintings on the history pages are the work of pioneer photographer and artist, William Henry Jackson.

Born in the state of New York, Jackson was a self-taught artist. He began his photography career working in a photographer's studio at the age of 15. Several years later he went to work for a studio in Vermont, only to leave, enlisting in the Union Army at the outset of the Civil War.

In 1866 Jackson moved west, where he witnessed many changes in American life and captured them with his camera lens and paint brush. In Nebraska, he worked as a bullwhacker for a freighting outfit bound for the goldfields of Montana. Traveling along the old trails, Jackson sketched the landmarks, sites and hardships experienced by westward-bound emigrants.

Mormon Trail History

"Emigrants at Kanesville"

MORMON TRAIL HISTORY

The following are excerpts from Mormon pioneer letters and diaries:

"I beheld the Saints coming in all directions from hills and dales, groves and prairies with their wagons, flocks and herds, by the thousands. It looked like the movement of a nation."

~ Unknown

"The place where we have settled for winter quarters is one of the most beautiful flats I've ever seen ... The scene is quite romantic."

~ Samuel Richards

"Although the river is wide and shallow, the water is the most beautiful that I have seen .."

~ Thomas Bullock

"... not a tree to shelter us from the scorching sun; it seemed that we must dissolve with the heat."

~ Louisa Pratt

"Had a buffalo fight in the river. Saw thousands of buffalo today which moved as black clouds in the prairie. It is a sight not to be described and only to be realized by the sight."

~ Hosea Stout

"We have been thrown like a stone from a sling and we have lodged in this goodly place just where the Lord wants his people to gather."

~ Brigham Young

"We made and broke the road from Nauvoo to this place. Some of the time we followed Indian trails; some of the time we ran by the compass; when we left the Missouri River we followed the Platte. And we killed rattlesnakes by the cord in some places; and made roads and built bridges till our backs ached. Where we could not build bridges across rivers, we ferried our people across."

~ Brigham Young

HISTORY OF THE MORMON TRAIL

THE MORMON TRAIL

The story of the Mormon Trail is one of hard workers and kind people. The Mormon exodus to the Salt Lake Valley was much more than a migration west; it was the movement of an entire people, their belongings and their beliefs.

The Mormon exodus is known as the largest, most organized and successful journey of a single group of people in United States history. The official commencement occurred on February 4, 1846, but the seeds were planted many years before ...

JOSEPH SMITH – THE FOUNDER, THE MARTYR

Joseph Smith was born in Sharon, Vermont, on December 23, 1805. As the fourth child in a farm family, no one predicted Smith would one day become the founding father of a religious movement and a martyr for his faith.

As a young teen, Smith announced he had received a heavenly manifestation. This manifestation led him to found the Mormon church in 1830 at the age of 25. This new church, in Palmyra, New York, drew many followers as well as many critics. Its converts, who referred to themselves as saints, were often the target of religious persecution.

Shortly after the church was organized, Smith and his followers were driven from New York. This was the first of many moves. The Mormons settled in Ohio, then in Missouri, and then in the Mississippi River town, Nauvoo, Illinois. It was in Illinois where Smith was murdered, becoming a martyr for his beliefs.

HISTORY OF THE MORMON TRAIL

BRIGHAM YOUNG – THE LEADER

With their founder gone, the Mormons needed to choose a new leader. Brigham Young, who served as the senior apostle of the church, was chosen to serve as the new president.

Young was born in Vermont in 1801, and in 1835, became a member of the church's original Quorum of the Twelve Apostles. The Mormon Trail, conceived by Joseph Smith, was carried out through Young. It was Young's desire to lead his people to a safe place where they would finally be free to follow the teachings of the church. His people had already moved too many times, having built homes and places of worship only to have them destroyed or left behind. But with the murder of Smith, it was once again evident they must flee. It was at this time, the Mormon Trail was born in the hearts and minds of the Mormon people.

This time, however, the move had to be far away. Young had read the report of explorer John Charles Fremont, who wrote of the valley of the Great Salt Lake. This was a place they could be away from all people; it wasn't even under the control of any nation or country. There the people would be free to worship – it would be a utopia! The Salt Lake Valley had been reported by trappers and explorers as a wild, desolate place. Young saw it as a place where, by the grace of God, the Mormons could settle and never have to move again. Young did not know exactly where in the valley they would settle, but he knew God would show him.

REQUIREMENTS FOR THE JOURNEY

Before the exodus began, a committee appointed by Brigham Young compiled the following list of required items for a family of five for the journey west:

Animals:
Two or three good milk cows
One or two good beef cows
Three sheep, if obtainable
Two or three good yoke of oxen, ages 4-10

HISTORY OF THE MORMON TRAIL

Food Items:

1,000 pounds flour in good sacks
One bushel beans
5 pounds dried peaches
A few pounds dried beef or bacon
5 pounds soda
One pound cinnamon
12 nutmegs, 25 pounds salt

25 pound sack grain
10 pounds dried apples
20 pounds dried pumpkin
100 pounds sugar
One pound cayenne
One-half pound cloves
2 pounds black pepper

Tools and Miscellaneous:

One good musket or rifle for each
   male over 12, with one pound powder
   and four pounds lead
One strong wagon, well covered
25-100 pounds farming and mechanical tools
Clothing and bedding, not to exceed 500 pounds

Cooking utensils: bake kettle, fry pan, tin
   cups, plates, forks, knives, spoons, pans, etc.
A few goods to trade with the Indians
15 pounds iron and steel
A few pounds wrought nails
One gallon alcohol, 20 pounds soap
One fish seine for every company,
   four or five hooks and lines

Supplies needed for multiple families or a company:

A good tent and furniture for every two families
One or more sets of saw and gristmill irons to every 100 families
Two sets of pulley blocks for crossing rivers to every company
Two ferry boats to every company, each wagon to carry 2,800 pounds
10 extra teams per company of 100

The committee also wrote:

"In addition to the above list, horse and mule teams can be used as well as oxen. Many items of comfort and convenience will suggest themselves to a wise and provident people, and can be laid in season, but none should start without filling the original bill first."

HISTORY OF THE MORMON TRAIL

THE MORMON TRAIL

On February 4, 1846, under the direction of Brigham Young, the first group left Illinois for the promised land. The next month, persecution caused more parties to leave for the West, and by September, all but 250 families had left their Nauvoo homes. The Mormon Trail blazed from Nauvoo, Illinois, to the Salt Lake Valley. The Trail was divided into two legs, 265 miles from Nauvoo to Winter Quarters, present-day Omaha, Nebraska, and 1,032 miles from there to present-day Salt Lake City, Utah.

Desiring to live among their fellow believers, Mormons from all over the world joined in the journey. Approximately 62,000 Mormon pioneers used the Trail from 1846 to 1869. On the journey, advance parties stopped periodically and made camps along the trail. The two major camps made in Iowa were Garden Grove and Mount Pisgah.

After crossing Iowa, they settled for the winter at Winter Quarters. From Winter Quarters they left in shifts for the West. For the next 23 years, the Mormon people continued to gather and come in shifts called companies. They traveled in this manner so the first people could break enough ground and plant enough crops to feed those that were coming later, warding off a food shortage.

Following the winter of 1846 spent at Winter Quarters, the first group, including Young, departed on the second leg of the journey on April 5, 1847. The group was well provisioned, including 72 wagons, 143 men, three women, two children, 93 horses, 66 oxen, 52 mules, 19 cows, 17 dogs, and some chickens. They expected to arrive in the Salt Lake Valley by mid-summer.

The Mormon people primarily traveled on the north side of the Platte River through Nebraska to avoid coming into contact with any other people, whom they called gentiles.

HISTORY OF THE MORMON TRAIL

Eventually, however, their path merged with the Oregon-California Trails at Fort Laramie, Wyoming. Here the Trail crossed over to the south side of the North Platte River until it reached the Sweetwater River at Casper, Wyoming. They followed this river until crossing the Continental Divide at South Pass. At Fort Bridger, the Mormon Trail broke away from the Oregon Trail and followed the faint, year-old Donner-Reed route through the Wasatch Mountains into the valley of the Great Salt Lake.

> "We could look forward for miles and behold the prairie spotted with wagons, cattle, horses and sheep, men, women and children." ~ Newel Knight

As they traveled, the Mormon people improved the Trail for those coming later. They built bridges and ferries, planted crops and built homes. When ferries were built, someone would stay behind to aid the following groups in crossing that particular river. They would allow other Mormons to use their improvements for free, but any others who happened to follow their Trail would be charged for using it. The money collected was sent back east to aid other groups of Mormons in gathering the needed supplies for their journey west. The first Mormon companies also planted crops periodically so others could harvest the crop when they got to it, thus boosting a possibly dwindling food supply.

The Mormon exodus was very successful in comparison to those of other pioneers traveling west for gold or land. In all, the Mormons lost 6,000 along the way, but this number is low compared to most other traveling groups. The Mormons did suffer from exposure to the elements and poor nutrition, but again, not as much as the other travelers.

Sod House

History of the Mormon Trail

The reason for this success was the organization of the Mormon people. Brigham Young and his council saw to every detail from food to daily schedules. People were organized in groups of 10, 50, and 100. They believed ultimately in community values and in community property. They had strict rules, which all the people followed for the benefit of themselves and the community.

A Typical Day on the Mormon Trail

The first winter spent at Winter Quarters gave Brigham Young much time to contemplate the upcoming journey. During this time, Young and the company captains mapped out the daily activities of the pioneers. The activities were designed to give the people energy through food and rest, time for proper care of their animals and personal belongings, and time to spend in worship and prayer.

A typical day followed this pattern:

5:00 a.m.	Bugle Call - Rise, pray, attend to the team, eat breakfast
7:00 a.m.	Depart on the day's journey
Noon	Stop for dinner, eat prepared food to make best use of the travel time
1:00 p.m.	Depart for the rest of the day's journey
Evening	Stop, draw up camp, eat supper
8:30 p.m.	Return to tents, pray
9:00 p.m.	In bed with fires out

On Saturday evenings, they would pitch camp and remain there until Monday morning, keeping Sunday as their day of worship and rest. Occasionally, the pioneers' mundane daily routine would be broken by the sighting of a landmark or an unusual occurrence such as seeing Indians, other travelers and buffalo herds.

HISTORY OF THE MORMON TRAIL

> "Thousands of buffalo could be seen. One day we could hear a roaring noise when they were miles away. They came straight for our train ... It was a fine sight to look at ... There was about five thousand of them. It took such a long time for them to pass ... Our cattle got so they could hardly be controlled. There were a good many stampedes." ~ Elizabeth Lamb

UTOPIA

The first party reached the Salt Lake Valley on July 22, 1847. Young was following two days behind this scouting party because of a bout with mountain fever. "It is enough. This is the right place," Young said when he viewed the Salt Lake Valley for the first time. Later, Young recorded the event in these words:

> "The spirit of light rested upon me and hovered over the valley, and I felt that there the Saints would find protection and safety." ~ Brigham Young

A few of those traveling with Young also made a record of this day in their diaries. Clara Decker Young said that when she heard Young, she was distraught, "... for it seemed to me the most desolate in all the world." Thomas Bullock shouted, "... hurra, hurra, hurra, there's my home at last."

With patience and hard work, this place became the utopia they, and thousands following after them, had longed for.

HISTORY OF THE MORMON TRAIL

HANDCART PIONEERS

"Let them come on foot with handcarts or wheelbar-rows; let them gird up their loins and walk through and nothing shall hinder or stay them."

~ Brigham Young

Heeding the rally cry of Brigham Young, impoverished Mormons who had previously considered settling in the Salt Lake Valley an unattainable dream, set out for the promised land. Unable to afford animals to pull wagons or even the wagons themselves, they prepared to walk the entire route pushing and pulling handcarts.

Companies using handcarts were formed during the middle part of the exodus as the result of a crop failure that left the church short of funds to buy wagons and oxen to bring them west.

Handcarts were small two-wheeled carts, modeled after carts used by street sweepers, that held a maximum load of 400 to 500 pounds. Pioneers heaped their possessions on the six to seven feet long cart and set out with the father and mother pulling while the children pushed behind.

The reason for using handcarts was twofold: to get to the Salt Lake Valley quickly and to save money. Handcart companies could travel 25-30 miles a day, where wagons could only travel 10-15 miles a day. However, the first groups paid a heavy price for mistakes in planning. Carpenters who made the carts used green lumber and dispensed with iron axles and tires to save expense and time. The cart's wooden axles were soon ground down by sand and cracked from the summer heat.

HISTORY OF THE MORMON TRAIL

Ten companies, primarily made of European converts, traveled between 1856 and 1860. In all, around 3,000 Mormons – approximately 300 people per company – with 653 carts and 50 supply wagons, traveled in this manner.

The handcarts were primarily successful, however two companies, Martin and Willie, started out too late in the fall, were caught in the mountains in winter and suffered greatly. Hundreds died from exposure and starvation. These handcart pioneers were finally rescued by Mormons who were already settled in Salt Lake City.

> "I have pulled my handcart when I was so weak and weary from illness and lack of food that I could hardly put one foot ahead of the other. I have looked ahead and seen a patch of sand or a hill slope and I have said, I can go only that far and there I must give up, for I cannot pull the load through it ... I have gone on to that sand and when I reached it, the cart began pushing me. I have looked back many times to see who was pushing my cart, but my eyes saw no one. I know then that the angels of God were there."
>
> ~ William Palmer,
> member of the Martin company

LANDMARKS ALONG THE MORMON TRAIL

Landmarks were used to gauge the remaining distance to the Salt Lake Valley, to provide a much-needed resting point and to search for signs or a note left by loved ones in the rare case that families traveled separately. For these reasons, an area normally considered ordinary was greatly awaited. Often upon reaching the landmark, the Mormon's spirits were uplifted, and they celebrated with music, prayer and dancing.

HISTORY OF THE MORMON TRAIL

Because improvements were made to the trail by earlier emigrants, many Mormon Trail landmarks were man-made. Several natural landmarks were shared with other trails after the merging point at Fort Laramie.

Garden Grove Way-Station

Located half-way between Nauvoo and Winter Quarters, Garden Grove, Iowa, served as a way station from 1846 until 1852. An early group camped and made improvements for those who would follow. Within two weeks of their arrival, the advance group cleared 300 acres, planted crops, built houses, and cut 10,000 rails for fencing and enough logs for 40 more houses.

Mount Pisgah Way-Station

Just a few miles west of Garden Grove, Mount Pisgah served the Mormon travelers until 1852. Here, all in one day, advance groups broke ground, planted crops and built homes for those who would follow. Mount Pisgah is located near present-day Thayer, Iowa.

Winter Quarters

The Indians granted the Mormons permission by a two-year treaty to establish a city and to graze their animals at a place just across the Missouri River from Cutler's Park. This place aptly became known as

Winter Quarters and served as the main headquarters of the Church during their migration west. Because of exhaustion, poor nutrition, disease and exposure to the elements, death claimed 600 during the first winter. The Mormon Pioneer Cemetery is located at Winter Quarters, found in present-day Omaha, Nebraska.

HISTORY OF THE MORMON TRAIL

"Had an opportunity of viewing the bank of the stream ... The opposite bluffs, rudely scalloped with shrubbery, presented a scene that might well be called wildly beautiful." ~ Eliza Snow

Kanesville

At the end of the two-year treaty, the town of Kanesville, Iowa, present-day Council Bluffs, was built up and populated by the Mormons. The region was cultivated to form a base for the westward march. They planted 4,000 acres of wheat, corn, potatoes and vegetables and built the town much like Winter Quarters.

Picture courtesy of Scotts Bluff National Monument

Emigrants at Kanesville

Elkhorn Ferry Crossing

The Elkhorn Ferry Crossing, located near present-day Elkhorn, Nebraska, was a designated gathering place and staging area for the Mormon travelers. This was the first major river crossing west of the Missouri River.

Genoa Way-Station

The Genoa Way-Station was built for freighting services in 1857. It provided a Loup River ferry crossing, a brick yard, saw mill, and thousands of acres of farmland. Although it only served until 1859, wagon wheel ruts can still be seen in this area, near present-day Genoa, Nebraska.

Lone Tree

As they traversed the rolling Nebraska prairies, the travelers awaited this giant, solitary cottonwood tree. The tree, near present-day Central City, Nebraska, punctuated the treeless landscape. Many travelers carved their initials in this lone tree. This was the most noted tree on the trail, however, the pioneers took special notice of any solitary tree.

HISTORY OF THE MORMON TRAIL

> *"Then we traveled miles without seeing a tree. When, at length, we came to a lone cedar tree, we stopped our teams, alighted, and many of the company walked quite a distance for the pleasure of standing a few moments under its branches."*
>
> ~ *Louisa Barnes Pratt*

Fort Kearny
Fort Kearny was established in 1848 to protect mail-carrying stages, and gold rush prospectors and miners. Fort Kearny, located near present-day Kearney, Nebraska, was long-awaited by the Mormons; it was here they could receive their first news from loved ones they may have left behind. Fort Kearny became a much-needed resting point.

Picture courtesy of Scotts Bluff National Monument

Fort Kearny

Odometer Start Point
On May 12, 1847, William Clayton first used his "roadometer," near present-day North Platte, Nebraska, consisting of wooden cogs geared to a wagon wheel. The odometer registered the distance traveled, enabling Clayton to tell how far they had gone. Previously, Clayton had kept track of distance by tying a red cloth to a wheel and counting its revolutions.

Ash Hollow
Although the Mormons entered Ash Hollow by means of the treacherous Windlass Hill, it provided much-needed visual relief after weeks of traveling the treeless prairie. This thick stand of ash trees near present-day Lewellen, Nebraska, was a welcome sight.

History of the Mormon Trail

Ancient Bluff Ruins and Ruts
English Mormons found these natural rock features to resemble the ruined castles of their homeland. They climbed the bluffs, near present-day Broadwater, Nebraska, wrote their names on buffalo skulls and were inspired to pray.

Courthouse and Jail Rocks
This visual illusion of two lone clay and sandstone rock uplifts located near present-day Bridgeport, Nebraska, seemingly changed shape as the travelers approached them. From far away, they thought these formations resembled a jail beside a courthouse.

Chimney Rock
Chimney Rock could be seen in the distance nearly a week before it was reached on foot. At 260 feet tall, it became the most noted landmark on the trail and received more diary space than any other place on the trail. Chimney Rock is located at present-day Bayard, Nebraska.

Chimney Rock

"Camped opposite Chimney Rock ... Here the scenery is remarkable, interesting and romantic. It produces an impression as if we were bordering on a large and antiquated city ..."
— Richard Ballantyne

HISTORY OF THE MORMON TRAIL

Scotts Bluff

This massive promontory rising 800 feet above the valley floor was named for Hiram Scott, a fur trapper who became ill, was abandoned by his companions and died near it in 1828. To the pioneers, Scotts Bluff marked the end of the Great American Desert and the beginning of the Rocky Mountains. Scotts Bluff is located near present-day Gering, Nebraska, where eroded wagon ruts are still visible.

Prayer Circle Hollow

After becoming disturbed by the behavior of some fellow Mormons, Brigham Young convened a prayer circle of a quorum of the twelve apostles of the Mormon church, in a hollow near present-day Henry, Nebraska. The time of prayer and the sermon he preached called the men to repentance and brought a "marvelous change" to all.

> *"Joking, nonsense, profane language, trifling conversation and loud laughter do not belong to us. Suppose the angels were witnessing the hoe-down the other evening, and listening to the haw haws ... would they not be ashamed of it?"*
>
> ~ Brigham Young

Fort Laramie

This early trading post, located at present-day Fort Laramie, Wyoming, was established in 1834, becoming the first garrisoned post in Wyoming and a key resupply point. It was here that the Mormon and Oregon-California trails merged, and the traveling saints merged with the gentiles.

Fort Laramie

Picture courtesy of Scotts Bluff National Monument

HISTORY OF THE MORMON TRAIL

Register Cliff

This cliff often served as a campsite used on the first day out from Fort Laramie, 11 miles away. Register Cliff served as a guestbook for all westward travelers. Often notes would be left on the cliff for those following behind, and later travelers would search the cliff for the signature of a loved one who had gone before. Several hundred names are still legible on Register Cliff, near present-day Guernsey, Wyoming.

Mormon Ferry

Established in June 1847, Mormon Ferry, located at present-day Casper, Wyoming, was the first commercial ferry on the Platte River. Mormon Ferry was owned and operated by the Mormon people.

Independence Rock

This rock formation was named on July 4, 1830, by fur trappers who first stopped at it to celebrate Independence Day. Located north of present-day Lamont, Wyoming, Independence Rock is where the Mormons reached the refreshing waters of the Sweetwater River.

> *"In advance of us, at a great distance can be seen the outlines of mountains, loftier than any we have yet seen ... their summits ... covered with snow."*
> ~ Horace Whitney

South Pass

Using South Pass, found west of present-day Atlantic City, Wyoming, the travelers were able to cross the Continental Divide on a gentle grade that was easy on the wagons.

HISTORY OF THE MORMON TRAIL

Picture courtesy of Scotts Bluff National Monument

Echo Canyon

Fort Bridger
Fort Bridger served as a station at the onset of the 1847 exodus and soon became a military post. The fort, located at present-day Fort Bridger, Wyoming, was built in 1842 by famous mountain man, fur trapper, Indian fighter and guide Jim Bridger and his partner Louis Vasques. It opened as a trading post in 1843 and was second only to Fort Laramie as an outfitting point.

Echo Canyon
This narrow 16-mile gorge impressed the travelers with its remarkable echo. Echo Canyon is just inside the Utah border near present-day Morgan, Utah.

Little Emigration Canyon
Little Emigration Canyon, located near present-day Salt Lake City, Utah, was the Mormons' last climb before reaching the Salt Lake Valley.

Salt Lake City
The utopia the travelers had been longing for stretched out for miles in front of them as they passed through Little Emigration Canyon – it was the end of the Mormon Trail.

Picture courtesy of Scotts Bluff National Monument

Salt Lake Valley

"... and beholding in a moment such an extensive scenery open before us, we could not refrain from a shout of joy which almost involuntarily escaped from our lips the moment this grand and lovely scenery was within our view." ~ Orson Pratt

Ethnic Cooking

"Sand Hills of the Platte Valley"

ETHNIC COOKING

Israel! Israel! Canst thou linger
Still in error's gloomy ways?
Mark how judgement's pointing finger
Justifies no vain delays.
Come to Zion, come to Zion!
Zion's walls shall ring with praise.
Come to Zion, come to Zion!
Zion's walls shall ring with praise.

~ excerpt from a poem by
Richard Smyth, immigrant
from Ireland in 1863

As the United States is the melting pot of the world, so was the Mormon Trail. Because of the Mormon's extensive mission efforts, their church was made up of people from many countries. From the founding of the church, Mormons had traveled the globe, bringing their message to people.

The Mormon exodus from Illinois to Utah brought members of the church from the United States and around the globe together to search for a place where they could be free to believe as they wished. This search brought together the people of many ethnic groups and the cooking traditions of each.

There is no typical Mormon cook. She was Swedish, Irish, German or from a myriad of other countries. She brought with her the cooking traditions and the methods of food preparation she had grown up with; she brought different tastes and different foods. Often a wealthy woman in her own country, she was thrust into a foreign culture, enduring a lifestyle far from what she was accustomed.

Many times, ingredients for cherished recipes could not be found in this new country, and Mormon cooks had to make do with what they could find. Using the fruits of this land, they tried to cure any homesickness by preparing the recipes of their old country.

This section is a celebration of ethnicity and ethnic cooking. It is a celebration of the ingenuity that was required of a Mormon cook, and of favorite recipes brought from an array of homelands.

Ethnic Cooking

German

Pig In The Blanket

1 round steak
Salt & pepper
1 med. onion

Bacon
1 c. beef broth

Cut steak into strips about 3 inches wide. Sprinkle steak with salt, pepper and onion. Place strip of bacon on meat. Roll up and skewer with toothpicks. Brown on medium heat. Once browned, thoroughly cover with beef broth. Simmer 3 hours or until tender. Remove meat and make gravy with drippings. May add water.

BIEROCKS
(Cabbage Rolls)

1 lg. head cabbage
2 lg. onions
2 lbs. ground beef

Shortening
Salt, pepper & celery salt to
  taste

Dough:

1 cake yeast
2 c. warm milk or water
½ c. sugar
½ c. shortening

1 tsp. salt
2 eggs, beaten
7 to 8 c. flour (or enough to
  make soft dough)

Chop cabbage and onion; set aside. Crumble meat in skillet and brown with salt, pepper and celery salt to taste. Remove meat and add enough shortening to make ½ cup. Saute onions in the shortening and then add them to the meat. Using a medium heat, cook the cabbage in the remaining shortening for about 15 minutes or until tender. Stir the cabbage often while cooking or it will burn. Mix with meat and onion; set aside to cool. Soften yeast in warm milk or water and mix in sugar, shortening, salt, egg and flour. Let rise until doubled in bulk. Punch down and let rise again. Turn out on board. Divide dough. Roll ½ of dough at a time to about ⅜ inch thick. Cut into 5 or 6-inch squares. Place portion of filling in center of squares and pull the corners together. Pinch opening securely. Turn pinched side down on cookie sheet or shallow pan. Grease generously and let rise until double in bulk. Bake at 425° until golden brown, about 20 minutes. Makes 24.

SAUERBRATEN WITH VEGETABLES

5-lb. pot roast of beef, round or rump	10 peppercorns
2 c. vinegar	2 bay leaves
2 c. water	1 lemon, sliced
1 onion, sliced	2 T. shortening
¼ c. honey	All-purpose flour
2 tsp. salt	Potatoes
	Carrots

Put meat in a large bowl. In a saucepan combine vinegar, water, onion, honey, salt, peppercorns and bay leaves. Bring to a boil. Cool and pour over meat. Add lemon. Cover and refrigerate for 3 days. Turn meat each day. Remove meat from marinade, reserving marinade, and dry with paper towels. Brown on all sides in shortening. Place on rack in roasting pan. Strain marinade and add 1½ cups to the meat. Add vegetables and simmer for 2½ to 3 hours or until tender. Allow 1 potato and 2 carrots per serving. Remove meat and vegetables and place on platter. Thicken gravy with flour mixed with a little cold water. Simmer for a few minutes; adjust seasoning. Makes 6 to 8 servings.

KARTOFFEL & KLOESSE
(German Potatoes & Dumplings)

2 eggs, beaten
Water (same amount as eggs),
  measure in egg shell
Salt to taste

1 to 1½ c. flour
Potatoes, cubed
Butter, melted

Beat the eggs. Add the water and salt. Stir in the flour to get dough as stiff as can be stirred with a spoon (but still very soft). Dough is stiff enough if it doesn't cling to the mixing bowl. Boil cubed potatoes until half done in lightly salted water, approximately 1 teaspoon. Drop dumpling dough from a moistened spoon into boiling water and potatoes, dipping spoon in the hot water each time. Cook 5 to 10 minutes until done. Drain water and save. Pour melted butter over potatoes and dumplings. Serve with sauerkraut or cream slightly diluted with the water drained from dumplings. To use leftover potatoes, boil the dumplings separately 5 to 10 minutes and brown lightly in butter with the potatoes.

GERMAN NOODLE RING
(With Cheese Sauce)

1 c. med. noodles, cooked,
  drained & rinsed
3 T. butter
3 T. flour
½ tsp. salt
½ tsp. paprika

1½ c. milk
6 to 8 oz. cheddar cheese, cut
  in pieces
2 eggs, well beaten
Vegetables

Spoon cooked noodles into buttered 1½-quart ring mold. Melt butter in saucepan. Blend in flour, salt and paprika. Heat until mixture bubbles, stirring constantly. Remove from heat. Add milk gradually, stirring until well blended. Bring rapidly to boiling, stirring constantly. Cook 1 to 2 minutes. Cool slightly; add cheese all at one time and stir rapidly until cheese is melted. Reserve ½ of sauce to use later. Add beaten eggs gradually to remaining sauce, blending well. Pour over noodles. Bake in boiling water bath about 40 minutes or until set. Unmold onto large platter. Pour remaining sauce over mold and fill center with desired vegetables, such as peas, carrots, spinach or asparagus tips. Makes approximately 8 servings.

KARTOFFEL PUFFER
(Potato Pancakes)

2 T. flour
1½ tsp. salt
¼ tsp. baking powder
⅛ tsp. pepper
2 eggs, beaten

1 T. grated onion
1 T. minced parsley
6 med. potatoes, grated
Shortening

Combine flour with salt, baking powder and pepper. Combine eggs, onion and parsley, and combine with the first mixture. Drain the potatoes that are grated and add to egg/flour mixture. Make into cakes and fry in ¼ inch melted shortening until brown.

German Slaw

1 sm. head cabbage	1 tsp. celery seed
2 med. onions, sliced	½ c. oil
1½ tsp. salt	½ c. vinegar
½ c. sugar	1 tsp. dry mustard

Shred cabbage and add onions. In saucepan combine salt, sugar, celery seed, oil, vinegar and mustard. Bring to a full rolling boil and pour over cabbage and onion. Stir well. Let stand 4 to 6 hours before serving.

Germanfest Pumpernickel Bread

1 T. yeast	2 T. caraway seed
¼ c. warm water	1 tsp. salt
⅓ c. brown sugar	2 c. boiling water
¼ c. rolled oats	3½ to 4 c. all-purpose flour
¼ c. shortening	2 c. rye flour
¼ c. molasses	

In small bowl stir together yeast and warm water. In a large bowl combine brown sugar, oats, shortening, molasses, caraway seed and salt. Pour boiling water over mixture. Stir and cool. Stir in yeast mixture. Beat in 2 cups all-purpose flour; stir in rye flour and as much white flour as able. Turn out on floured surface, kneading in more flour to make a moderately stiff dough. Knead until smooth and elastic, about 10 minutes. Shape into a ball and place in greased bowl. Turn to grease surface of dough. Cover and let rise until doubled, about 1 hour. Punch down; shape into 2 round loaves. Place on greased baking sheet. Flatten into 6-inch rounds. Cover and let rise until doubled, about 1 hour. Bake at 375° for 35 to 40 minutes or until bread sounds hollow when tapped. Cool on wire rack.

NORWEGIAN

NORWEGIAN KALDALMER

½ lb. ground pork
½ lb. ground beef
1 med. onion, chopped
1 c. cream
3 T. butter

1 egg
2 T. flour
2 T. raw rice
1 med. cabbage head
1 c. tomato juice

Mix all ingredients except cabbage and tomato juice. Wrap into cabbage leaves. Place in pan and pour tomato juice over all. Bake 1 hour.

RULLE POLSE
(Norwegian Meat Roll)

2½ lbs. flanks of beef
1 lb. beef
½ lb. pork
¼ lb. finely ground beef
¼ lb. finely ground pork

3 T. minced onion
1 T. pepper
1 T. ginger
4 T. salt

Trim all fat and sinews from flank. Flatten on a board. Rub in pan of pepper, ginger and salt. Add remainder of seasoning mixture and onion to the ground meat. Spread beef and pork on a little more than half of flank. Spread ground seasoned meat on top. Roll tightly and sew edges together to keep stuffing inside. Wrap tightly in a cloth. Put in a pot and cover with water. Cook slowly for about 2 to 3 hours. Remove from pot. Place between plates under a heavy weight to press out moisture until the roll is cold. Remove cloth and slice thin. Remove threads and serve cold. Keep cool until ready to serve.

KUMPS
(Norwegian Potato Dumplings)

8 c. ground raw potatoes
2 c. ground cooked potatoes
5 c. flour
1 tsp. baking powder

2 tsp. salt
Salt pork or bacon that has
  been cut into sm. pieces
Ham broth

Mix all ingredients except meat and form into dumplings roughly the size of a medium to large potato. In center of each dumpling, put salt pork or bacon pieces. Cook one hour in a boiling ham broth. Serve with boiled ham. **Optional:** A little ham broth mixed with melted butter can be used as a sauce over the Kumps.

SOT SUPPE
(Sweet Soup)

3 c. apple juice
½ c. dried apricots
¼ c. golden raisins
⅓ c. sugar
1 (3-in.) cinnamon stick

2 med. apples, peeled & finely
  chopped
1 tsp. grated lemon peel
4½ tsp. cornstarch
2 T. sliced almonds

In a large saucepan combine 2½ cups apple juice with the apricots, raisins, sugar, cinnamon stick, apples and lemon peel. Bring to a boil over medium heat. Reduce heat and simmer for 10 minutes or until apricots are tender. In a small bowl combine remaining ½ cup apple juice and cornstarch; stir into soup. Stirring constantly, cook for 3 or 4 minutes or until soup is slightly thickened. Remove cinnamon stick. Garnish each serving with sliced almonds. Serve leftover soup chilled for breakfast. Serves 4 to 5.

EASY OSTAKAKA

2 c. fine curd cottage cheese
6 eggs, beaten well
¾ c. sugar

3 c. cream
½ tsp. vanilla
½ tsp. almond extract

Combine all ingredients and mix well. Bake ½ hour at 300°. (Use deep pan; spatters greatly when baking.) Serve with berries on top.

SCANDINAVIAN SNOWBALLS

1 c. butter, softened
3 T. confectioners sugar
1 tsp. vanilla extract
½ tsp. almond extract

2 c. sifted flour
1 c. chopped blanched
  almonds
Confectioners sugar

Cream butter and sugar together until light and fluffy. Add vanilla and almond extracts. Stir in flour and almonds; dough will be quite stiff. Chill in a covered container. Form into small balls and bake on a baking sheet at 350° for 15 minutes or until golden brown. Cool and roll a couple of times in confectioners sugar. Makes 5 to 6 dozen.

NORWEGIAN BUTTER COOKIES

¾ c. butter
½ c. sugar
1 egg
1 tsp. vanilla

1 tsp. baking powder
1 c. flour
¾ c. cornstarch

Melt butter and cool until lukewarm. Add sugar and beat well. Add well-beaten egg, vanilla and dry ingredients sifted together. Drop by spoonfuls 2 or 3 inches apart. Bake at 350°.

SWEDISH

SWEDISH MEATBALLS

2 lbs. ground beef
1 lb. ground pork
5 slices wheat bread (no crust)
Milk or cream
2 eggs

1 med. onion, grated finely
½ tsp. allspice
¼ tsp. nutmeg
1 tsp. salt
½ tsp. pepper

Mix together the ground beef and pork. Crumble the bread slices in a bowl and add just enough milk (or cream) to soften. Add egg; stir until mushy. Add grated onion, spices, salt and pepper. Roll into small balls and bake on a jellyroll pan at 350° for 30 minutes. Stir and bake about 30 minutes more or until cooked through. Make a cream sauce and pour over the meatballs.

KORV
(Swedish Potato Sausage)

2½ lbs. ground pork
½ lb. ground beef
6 raw potatoes, peeled &
  coarsely ground
1 c. milk, scalded
1 med. size onion, peeled &
  ground

1 tsp. black pepper
2 T. salt
¾ tsp. allspice
2 tsp. ground ginger
Casings

Mix all ingredients together very thoroughly. Stuff into casings that expand to about 1¼ to 1½ inches when stuffed. Put in large roaster; prick the casings. Add enough water to make some steam. Bake until done at 350°, approximately 40 minutes. Makes 8 rings, approximately ¾ pound each.

SWEDISH HEAD CHEESE

3 lbs. pork shank   2 pigs feet
1 lb. veal shank   Salt & pepper
2 lbs. beef shank

Boil meat all together; cool. Slice into cubes. Put in cloth and season with salt and pepper. Pour the hot liquid, in which it was cooked, over it and let stand in a pan with a heavy weight on it. When it is pressed, take it out of the cloth and put in a crock of brine.

LEFSE

2 c. potatoes, cooked & cubed   2 T. butter
¼ c. cream   1 tsp. sugar
1 tsp. salt   1 c. flour

Mash potatoes with cream, salt, butter and sugar. Add enough flour to make dough stiff enough to roll. Shape into long roll. Cut off a small amount; roll on lightly floured board, keeping each cake as round as possible. Bake slowly on ungreased moderately hot griddle or heavy frying pan, turning to brown both sides. The cakes will blister and brown in spots. Remove from griddle; fold across middle twice to form a quarter circle. Serve as bread or with fish dinner, especially with lutefish.

SWEDISH RYE BREAD

1 cake yeast	1 T. fennel seed
½ c. + 1 T. sugar, divided	2½ c. rye flour
2½ c. warm water, divided	2 T. shortening
¼ c. molasses	½ c. brown sugar
1 to 2 tsp. salt	White flour

Dissolve yeast and 1 tablespoon sugar in ½ cup warm water; set aside. Mix all remaining ingredients with yeast mixture; blend well, adding small amounts of white flour until dough is soft and pliable. Knead and place in greased bowl. When dough has doubled in size, punch down; repeat. Let dough stand 20 minutes. Divide dough into thirds and place in loaf pans. Let rise again until doubled in bulk. Bake in a slow oven, 300°-325°, for 45 minutes.

SWEDISH ALMOND RUSKS

1 c. sugar (scant cup)	½ tsp. soda
½ c. butter	½ tsp. salt
1 egg	½ c. sour cream
1½ tsp. almond extract	½ c. chopped almonds
2½ c. flour	

Cream sugar and butter. Add egg and extract; beat. Mix all dry ingredients together; add them alternately to the above with sour cream. Add nuts. Divide dough into two rolls (10 to 12 inches long and 2 to 3 inches high). Place on cookie sheet and bake at 325° for 25 to 30 minutes. When baked, remove to a cutting board and slice ¼ to ⅛ inch thick. Place sliced pieces on cookie sheet. Dry out in the oven, until light brown, at 200°. Keep in covered container.

DANISH

DANISH MEATBALLS

1½ lbs. ground beef
½ lb. ground sausage
2 T. bread crumbs
1 egg
1 grated onion

¼ tsp. pepper
2 T. flour
1 tsp. salt
½ tsp. cloves
½ c. milk

Combine meat and bread crumbs. Add egg, onion, pepper, flour, salt and cloves, if desired. Add milk, a little at a time, mixing thoroughly. Let stand 3 hours. Drop from large tablespoon or roll into 1-inch diameter balls and cook in greased frying pan. May be served with or without gravy.

BALKEN BRIJ

1 lb. fat pork
2 lbs. pork liver
1 T. salt
Water

2 c. buckwheat flour
1 c. flour
Pepper
Shortening

Cook pork and liver slowly with salt until well done, approximately 1½ hours. Grind meat finely. Mix meat in pan with 6 pints water; heat. Mix in flours and pepper. Stir until thickened to a consistency that will drop off spoon. Put in loaves and keep chilled. Slice as needed and fry slices until brown on both sides in a frying pan with very little shortening. Serve as a breakfast dish in place of bacon or sausage.

AEBLESKIVERS
(Danish Pancake Balls)

2 c. flour
½ tsp. salt
1½ tsp. baking soda
1 tsp. baking powder
2 c. buttermilk

3 eggs, separated
1 tsp. vanilla
3 T. melted butter
Shortening

Sift flour, salt, baking soda and baking powder into bowl. Add buttermilk, egg yolks and vanilla; mix thoroughly. Beat egg whites until stiff, but not dry; fold into batter. Add butter; mix gently. Let stand about 30 minutes so that air bubbles can escape. Batter can be cooled for 2 days. Makes about 27 or 30 balls. **To Cook:** It is necessary to use a heavy, cast-iron Aebleskiver pan. Lighter aluminum pans tend to overheat and burn. Preheat the pan to a medium heat. The Aebleskiver pan generally has about 7 semi-spherical cavities. Add about ½ to 1 teaspoon of shortening to each cavity. If it sizzles, the pan is ready. Add enough batter to each cavity to fill to barely even with the top. As the batter begins to cook, a thin crust will begin to form at the sides of the cavities. Using a metal crochet hook, knitting needle or small skewer, prick the forming crust and gently rotate the cooking ball slightly. Continue to rotate in small increments until a complete ball is formed and the entire surface is golden brown. Getting the heat of the pan adjusted properly is important. If too hot, the outside will cook too quickly, may burn and the center will be raw. When properly cooked, remove from pan and place on platter. Dust liberally with powdered sugar. Aebleskivers may be covered with maple or fruit syrup or berry jam and eaten with sausage, bacon, ham, etc.

"They have so much of the spirit of gathering that they would go if they knew they would die as soon as they got there or if they knew that the mob would be upon them and drive them as soon as they got there."
~ Brigham Young

KRINGLER

4 c. flour
½ c. sugar
¼ tsp. salt
1 tsp. soda

1 c. butter
2 c. sour cream
Flour
Egg whites, beaten
Sugar

Sift together flour, sugar, salt and soda. Cut butter into dry ingredients like pastry. Add sour cream and additional flour to make soft dough to roll. Cut in strips ½ inch wide x 9 inches long. Form a figure 8. Dip in beaten egg whites and sprinkle with sugar. Bake at 400°.

DANISH PUFF

Puff:

1 c. sifted flour
½ c. butter

2 T. water

Topping:

½ c. butter
1 c. water
1 tsp. almond flavoring

1 c. sifted flour
3 eggs

Measure first cup of flour into bowl. Cut in butter. Sprinkle with 2 tablespoons water and mix with fork. Round into a ball and divide in half. Pat dough with hands into 2 strips (12 x 3 inches). Strips should be 3 inches apart on an ungreased baking sheet. Mix second amount of butter and water in pan and bring to a rolling boil. Add almond flavoring and remove from heat. Stir in flour immediately, all at once, to keep it from lumping. Add 1 egg at a time, beating until smooth. Divide in half and spread one-half on each piece of pastry. Bake 60 minutes in 350° oven. When cool, frost with confectioners' sugar icing and sprinkle with finely chopped nuts.

IRISH

Corned Beef & Cabbage

5 lbs. corned beef
Cold water to cover
2 lg. onions, sliced
2 lg. carrots, sliced

4 potatoes, peeled & sliced
1 lg. cabbage, quartered
Bay leaf
Black pepper

Cover the meat with water and bring to boil. Skim fat off the surface. Add the vegetables, except cabbage, bay leaf and pepper, and simmer gently for 90 minutes. Add cabbage, bay leaf and pepper. Cook 30 minutes longer. Serve the meat surrounded by the vegetables.

IRISH LAMB STEW

2 lbs. cubed lamb shoulder
1 gal. water
½ T. salt
1 c. chicken broth
1¼ tsp. black pepper
2 c. coarsely diced carrots
2 c. coarsely diced celery
1 leek, trimmed, washed &
  thinly sliced

3 med. green bell peppers,
  cored, seeded & diced
2 c. sweet white whole onions,
  cooked
2 c. cooked Irish potatoes
½ lb. butter
¾ c. flour

Add lamb to 2 quarts water; bring to boil. When the water comes to a boil, pour it off. Add 2 more quarts of water to the lamb along with the salt, chicken broth and pepper. Bring to boil, then add carrots, celery, leek and green pepper. Reduce to simmer and cook 20 minutes. Add onions and potatoes. Simmer 10 to 15 minutes or until lamb is tender. Melt butter in saucepan over medium heat. Stir in flour. Remove meat and vegetables from broth. Add the butter/flour mixture to the broth and stir over medium heat until the broth thickens. Return meat and vegetables to sauce and simmer until heated through. Serves 6.

PASTIES

Rich pastry (enough for a
  double-crust pie)
2 med. potatoes, sliced
1 med. onion, sliced
2 turnips, if desired

Salt & pepper to taste
Generous amount of parsley
¾ lb. beef
Water

Roll out pastry in square shape or long oval. Cover half of it with a
layer of sliced potatoes and a layer of onions. Add layer of turnips.
Add salt, pepper and parsley; sprinkle with water. Lay strips of meat
(size of finger) over top and around sides of vegetables. Fold other
half of pastry over meat and vegetables, forming a triangle and crimp
well. May also be made in individual sized servings. Slit a few vents
in the top of pastry and bake at 450° for 10 minutes. Reduce heat to
350° and continue baking for about 50 minutes.

COLCANNON
(Irish Potatoes)

6 med. potatoes, peeled &
  quartered
4 T. butter
4 c. cabbage, coarsely cut
½ tsp. salt, divided

½ tsp. pepper
½ to 1 c. green onions, sliced
¾ c. milk, warmed
Chopped parsley

In a large saucepan combine potatoes with water to cover and salt.
Bring to a boil; cover and cook until fork-tender, about 20 minutes.
Meanwhile, in medium skillet melt 2 tablespoons butter over low heat.
Add cabbage, ¼ teaspoon salt and pepper. Cook, stirring until tender,
about 10 to 12 minutes. Add onions; cover and set aside. Drain potatoes.
Mash until smooth. Add remaining butter and ¼ teaspoon of salt. Beat
in warm milk until fluffy. Fold in cabbage and onions. Makes about
6 cups.

34

Irish Soda Bread

3 c. flour
½ c. sugar
3¾ tsp. baking powder
½ tsp. salt

1 egg
1 c. plus 2 T. milk
1 c. raisins
3 T. melted butter

Sift together flour, sugar, baking powder and salt. Mix in egg and milk until well mixed. Stir in raisins. Add melted butter. Pour batter in loaf pan. Bake at 350° for 1 hour.

SCOTTISH

Winter Lamb Stew With Lentils & Mint

1 lb. lamb neck, chopped
4 qt. water
½ lb. dried lentils
4 carrots, cut in wedges or
  slices
White beans, cooked
4 red potatoes
1 to 2 tsp. salt to taste
4 yellow onions, coarsely
  chopped

4 T. shortening
1 bunch fresh mint leaves,
  washed & stemmed
¼ c. hot beef stock
1 T. brown sugar
6 lg. cloves garlic
2 to 3 T. flour

Bring the lamb and water to a boil in a large pot. Reduce to a simmer. Cook 15 minutes and add dried lentils. Cook 30 minutes and when lentils are tender, add carrots, white beans, potatoes and 1 teaspoon salt. In a skillet saute chopped onions in 2 tablespoons shortening until golden and soft. Add mint leaves; stir and let rest 5 minutes, then add to the pot. Add beef stock, sugar and chopped garlic. Cook flour in the last 2 tablespoons of shortening. Whisk hot broth into the cooked flour, then return to the pot. Simmer on low for 30 minutes, then serve.

Grilled Butterflied Leg Of Lamb

1 c. red wine vinegar
¾ c. soy sauce
4 cloves garlic, crushed
½ c. fresh mint leaves

2 T. rosemary leaves
1 T. ground black pepper
4 to 5-lb. butterflied leg of
  lamb

Combine vinegar, soy sauce, garlic, mint, rosemary and pepper in a
small bowl; mix well. Place lamb in baking dish. Pour mixture over
lamb. Cover and chill for 6 hours, turning lamb frequently. Drain meat;
reserve marinade, grill lamb, basting frequently about 20 minutes each
side. Check lamb for doneness after 30 minutes. Cut lamb into thin
slices.

Scottish Oat Cakes

1 c. oats
½ c. flour
1 T. sugar
¾ tsp. salt

⅛ tsp. baking soda
⅛ c. shortening
½ c. hot water

Mix oats, flour, sugar, salt and soda. Melt fat in hot water; add to oat
mixture. Mix thoroughly until thickens. Roll out on floured board as
thin as possible. Cut in strips. Bake at 350° for 30 to 35 minutes.

SCOTTISH OAT SCONES

²/₃ c. butter, melted
¹/₃ c. milk
1 egg
1¹/₂ c. flour
1¹/₂ c. quick oats, uncooked

¹/₄ c. sugar
1 T. baking powder
1 tsp. cream of tartar
¹/₂ tsp. salt
¹/₂ c. raisins

Add butter, milk and egg to combined flour, oats, sugar, baking powder, cream of tartar and salt. Mix just until dry ingredients are moistened. Stir in raisins. Shape dough to form ball. Pat out on a lightly greased sheet to form an 8-inch circle. Cut into 8 to 12 wedges. Bake at 425° for 12 to 15 minutes or until light brown. Serve warm with butter or preserves as desired.

SCOTTISH SHORTBREAD

1 c. butter
¹/₂ c. sugar

2 c. flour

Cream butter and sugar; add flour. Press into greased 8 x 12-inch baking pan. Bake at 350° for 30 minutes. Remove from heat and cut into squares while hot.

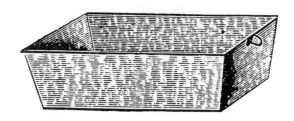

ENGLISH

BEEF ROAST WITH YORKSHIRE PUDDING

Beef roast with salt & pepper
  to taste
Water
2 eggs
2 c. sour milk

1 c. milk
2 tsp. baking powder
1 tsp. salt
1 T. sugar
2 c. flour (to make stiff batter)

Place roast in large pan. Add enough water to surround roast to at least ½ inch deep. Cover and bake until tender. Mix eggs, sour milk, milk, baking powder, salt, sugar and flour to make a stiff batter. When roast is done, check broth to be sure there's enough to cook the batter. Add batter to broth and around the roast. Cook for about 30 minutes longer at 350° or until the batter is a biscuit-like texture.

SHEPHERD'S PIE

½ c. onion, chopped
½ clove garlic
½ c. celery, chopped
½ c. green pepper, chopped
2 lbs. ground beef, lamb or
  turkey
1½ c. potatoes, mashed
1 c. water

2 c. green peas
1 T. butter
1 tsp. soy sauce
1 tsp. salt
Dash black pepper
⅓ c. cheese, shredded

Heat skillet. Saute onion, garlic, celery and green pepper until tender.
Add ground meat; scramble and cook until golden brown. Drain off
excess liquid. Using a small pot, boil 1 cup water and dash of salt.
Add green peas and bring to a boil. Let stand 2 minutes; strain. In
baking dish put cooked ground meat and vegetables. Add drained green
peas. Season poatoes with butter, soy sauce and salt. Top meat and
vegetables with potato mixture. Top potatoes with cheese. Bake in
350° oven until golden brown. Serves 8.

ENGLISH TEA BISCUITS

2 c. flour
4 tsp. baking powder
½ tsp. salt

2 tsp. shortening
¾ c. milk

Sift flour, baking powder, salt and add shortening, cutting it into dry
ingredients. Add milk. Roll and pat out to ½-inch thickness. Cut with
biscuit cutter and place in greased pan. Bake 10 minutes at 500°.

ENGLISH TOFFEE

1 lb. butter
¼ c. water
2 c. sugar

1 lb. finely chopped nuts
1 lb. milk chocolate

Melt butter. Add water and sugar. (One-third cup of nuts may be added to sugar and butter mixture and boiled right along with it.) Bring to a rolling boil, stirring constantly. Let it boil until it becomes a caramel color. Pour thinly on cookie sheets. Do not scrape sides of pan while pouring, as this causes butter and sugar to separate. Let cool, then spread both sides with chocolate and sprinkle with nuts.

WELSH

WELSH RAREBIT

¼ c. butter
5 T. flour
½ tsp. salt
2 c. milk
¼ tsp. Worcestershire sauce

½ lb. sharp cheese
1 egg, beaten
5 slices hot toast
Paprika

Make a white sauce with butter, flour, salt and milk. Add Worcestershire sauce and diced or grated cheese; stir until melted over low heat. Pour in well-beaten egg and continue cooking 1 minute, stirring constantly. Serve immediately over toast. Sprinkle with paprika, if desired. Makes 5 servings.

Welsh Cabbage Casserole

1 lb. cooked sausage
2 c. cooked, chopped cabbage
4 T. butter
4 T. flour

2 c. milk
Salt
Pepper
Bread crumbs

Line casserole with sausage. Spread cabbage on top. Melt butter in small heavy pan; blend in flour until smooth over low heat. Stir milk in slowly. Cook over low heat, stirring constantly, to boiling point. Cook 2 minutes until thick. Pour over the sausage and cabbage mixture. Season with salt and pepper to taste; sprinkle bread crumbs on top. Bake at 350° for 30 minutes. Serves 4 to 6.

FRENCH

FRENCH BEEF RAGOUT CREPES

12 to 14 cooked crepes
2 T. butter
3 T. shortening
2 strips bacon
1 c. sliced mushrooms
1 c. finely chopped onions
½ c. thinly sliced parsnips

1 lb. stew meat, cut into ¼-in. cubes
1 T. flour
1 tsp. salt
½ clove garlic, mashed
½ c. beef stock
⅔ c. red wine vinegar

Combine butter, shortening and bacon in large pan. Cook over low heat until bacon is transparent. Add mushrooms and cook, stirring over brisk heat 3 to 4 minutes. Remove mushrooms to a side dish. Using the same pan, add fat and drippings; saute onions and parsnips until golden brown. Add meat, flour, salt and garlic. Cook over high heat 3 to 4 minutes or until meat is nicely browned. Add stock and vinegar. Bring to a boil. Cover pan; reduce heat and simmer 45 to 55 minutes or until meat is tender. Add reserved mushrooms. Place a portion of this mixture on center of each crepe. Roll up crepes and place in layers in buttered baking dish. Pour any remaining gravy over crepes. Bake in 375° oven for 10 to 15 minutes. Serve at once. Serves 6.

CREPES

1½ c. milk   1 T. shortening
1 c. flour   ¼ tsp. salt
2 eggs

In a bowl combine milk, flour, eggs, shortening and salt. Beat until
well mixed. Heat a lightly greased 6-inch skillet. Remove from the
heat. Spoon in 2 tablespoons of the batter; lift and tilt the skillet to
spread batter. Return to heat; brown on one side only; remove crepe.
Repeat with remaining batter, greasing skillet occasionally. Makes 18.

FRENCH ONION SOUP

2 T. butter   1 tsp. Worcestershire sauce
2 c. thinly sliced onions   4 to 6 slices bread, toasted
4 c. beef broth   ¾ to 1 c. shredded cheese

In a large saucepan melt butter. Stir in onions. Cook, covered, over
medium-low heat for 8 to 10 minutes or until tender and golden, stirring
occasionally. Add beef broth, Worcestershire sauce and dash of pepper.
Bring to boiling; reduce heat. Cover and simmer for 10 minutes. Sprinkle toasted bread with cheese. Broil until cheese melts and turns light
brown. To serve, ladle soup into bowls and float bread atop.

Unforgettable Chocolate Mousse

6 oz. semi-sweet chocolate
1 T. orange juice
2 egg yolks
2 whole eggs

1 tsp. vanilla
¼ c. sugar
1 c. cream

Melt chocolate in orange juice over low heat; set aside. Blend egg yolks, whole eggs, vanilla and sugar. Add cream; blend 30 seconds. Add chocolate mixture; blend until smooth. Pour in serving cups.

Chocolate Eclairs

1 c. water
½ c. butter

1 c. flour
4 eggs

Heat water and butter to a rolling boiling point in saucepan. Stir in flour all at once. Stir vigorously over low heat until mixture leaves the pan and forms a ball (about 1 minute). Remove from heat. Add eggs, one at a time, beating after each. Beat mixture until smooth and velvety. Form into 4 x 1-inch fingers on ungreased pan. Bake at 400° for 45 to 50 minutes. Fill with Custard Filling.

Custard Filling:

½ c. sugar
½ tsp. salt
6 T. flour

2 c. milk
4 egg yolks or 2 eggs, beaten
2 tsp. vanilla

In a saucepan mix together sugar, salt and flour. Stir in milk. Cook over low heat, stirring until it boils. Boil 1 minute. Remove from heat. Stir a little of the mixture into the eggs. Blend in hot mixture in saucepan. Bring to a boiling point. Cool and blend in vanilla. Cut eclairs lengthwise. Fill with custard. Put chocolate icing on top. Chill.

DUTCH

Olie Bollen
(Dutch Donuts)

Sift Together:

2 c. flour
¼ c. sugar
3 tsp. baking powder

1 tsp. salt
1 tsp. nutmeg

Add:

¼ c. shortening
¾ c. milk
1 egg

1 c. raisins
1 c. apple, chopped (may be
   added)

Stir with fork until thoroughly mixed. Drop by teaspoon into hot fat. Fry until golden brown; drain. Roll warm puffs in cinnamon sugar mixture. Makes 30 puffs or Olie Bollen.

Bonquet

Dough:

1 lb. butter
4 c. flour

1 c. milk

Filling:

1 lb. almond paste
2 c. sugar

3 eggs
1 tsp. almond extract

Mix butter and 4 cups flour. Stir in milk; mix well. Chill overnight. Beat almond paste until smooth. Add sugar, eggs and extract; mix well and chill. Divide dough in 8. Roll out each to about 3 inches wide and 14 inches long. Take filling about thumb size; place on dough. Lap one side dough over filling, then fold over other side. Pinch ends. Place on greased sheet with seams on bottom. Brush tops with egg white. Prick with fork, 2 inches apart. Bake at 400° for 30 minutes.

Windmill Cookies

1 c. butter
1 c. sugar
1 egg, separated
2 c. flour

1½ to 2 tsp. cinnamon
½ tsp. salt
1 T. water
1 c. chopped nuts

Cream butter and sugar; add egg yolk. Sift flour, cinnamon and salt; add to cream mixture a little at a time. Drop dough in lumps in an oblong pan. Pat into thin layer. Blend water and egg white; stir until syrupy but not foamy. Pour over cookie dough. Tilt pan in all directions until dough is well coated. Sprinkle with nuts over top. Bake at 300° for 30 minutes. Remove from heat and let set for 15 minutes. Cut into bars or squares.

Preserving & Drying

"Fort Kearny"

Preserving & Drying

The preservation and drying of meats, fruits and vegetables was always an important part of pioneer cooking. However, when the Mormon pioneers began preparing for departure, preserving and drying became essential.

Following the directions of Brigham Young, the pioneers dried beef, pork, apples, peaches, beans and pumpkin. Young expected to find an abundance of wildlife and wild food in the land they would be crossing, so they prepared only basic food items in advance. The pioneers succeeded in living off the land, eating wild game, fish, fruits and vegetables. The food they prepared in advance was high in nutritional value, providing the needed variety to make meals tasty as well as satisfying.

The packing of food for traveling was nearly as important as what was packed. The food containers had to be sturdy, small, compact, waterproof, lightweight and easily secured. Dried fruits and vegetables kept in bags traveled much better than foods in crocks or jars, so they were much preferred over canned or pickled foods.

The Mormon pioneers took advantage of every opportunity to preserve food along the trail. Occasionally, they would experience a surplus of wild food. At these times, they would preserve the food so it could be used in case of a shortage later.

Mormon pioneer Elizabeth Lamb recorded the following about the advantageous use of the buffalo herds they encountered.

> "We had some of their meat. It was fine. We could
> cut it in slices, salt it, string it on sticks and jerk
> it over the fire to let it dry. It was sweet and good.
> We were in a wild country."
>
> ~ Elizabeth Lamb

The pioneers dried meats, fruits and vegetables along the trail. At times, fruits would be made into jams, jellies, cider and fruit butter. Although dried fruits and vegetables traveled best, jams and jellies satisfied the sweet tooth and gave the pioneers the extra boost of energy they often needed to complete a hard task on the trail.

PRESERVING & DRYING

CURED MEAT - BRINED MEAT

Rub meat well with salt; drain overnight to draw out blood. Make a brine as follows: For 100 pounds of meat, use 8 pounds salt, 2 pounds brown sugar, 2 ounces saltpeter and 4 gallons of boiling water. Dissolve all ingredients well in boiling water and cool. Pack meat in jars or barrels and cover with cold brine. The amount of salt varies a little for sugar cured ham and bacon. If meat is to be cured in warm weather, more salt should be used. Nine or ten pounds of salt might be safer in this case. If a mild cure is preferred and the meat is not to be kept very long, less salt or 8 pounds is recommended as in recipe above. Bacon strips should remain in the brine from 4 to 6 weeks. If the brine becomes ropy, take out all the meat and place in the brine again. Be sure that the brine covers the meat and that the meat is weighted down. In about 10 days, move the pieces about in the container, taking off brine, if necessary. This seems to give a little more even cure if done several times. Elk, venison and beef are all good cured in this brine. **Note:** If pork is cured, it may then be taken out and smoked in a smoke house. Use ash or apple wood to make a heavy, dense smoke. Mutton may also be used.

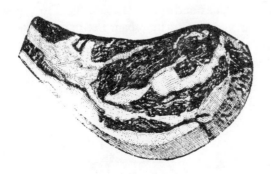

PIONEER PICKLED PIGS FEET

Pigs feet
Salt
Vinegar
Sugar

Pepper
Cinnamon
Cloves

Clean and scrape pigs feet thoroughly. Cut in halves lengthwise, then in 3 or 4 pieces. Cook in salt water until tender. Pack loosely in a crock. Cook vinegar (enough to cover) with ½ cup sugar to a quart. Add spices to taste. Pour boiling solution over prepared pigs feet. Place a plate with weight on it on crock. Let stand in cool place one week before using.

JELLIED PIGS FEET

4 pigs feet, cut in halves
2 pork shanks
1 onion, well browned
5 whole peppers

5 whole allspice
4 bay leaves
1 T. vinegar

Wash feet and shanks. Place in large kettle and cover with water. Bring to boiling point and skim. Add onion and spices; cover and simmer very slowly about 4 hours or until meat comes off bones easily. Cool, strain, remove the bones and spices. Return meat to liquid. Add salt and vinegar. Pour into loaf or tube pan. Set in cool place until firm. Scrape fat from top. Garnish with cooked carrot slices and hard cooked eggs.

Pioneer Pickled Buffalo
Or Beef Tongue

Makes approximately 3 pounds beef tongue. Boil tongue approximately 4 hours or until tender. When cool, the rough may be removed with a sharp knife. Slice and soak in cold water for one hour. Skin when cooked. Mix in saucepan:

2 c. water   **2 T. pickling spice**
2 c. vinegar   **1 tsp. salt**
1 T. vinegar

Bring to boil. Pour over drained beef tongue. One large onion may be sliced and added.

Bugle Call Cured Ham & Bacon

Salt   **Ham**
Water   **Bacon**

1¾ pounds salt to 1 gallon water for hams and 2 pounds salt to 1 gallon water for bacon. Let soak in crock for 1 week. String and smoke about a week or more.

Corned Bear Meat

50 lbs. bear meat	2 T. soda
2 lbs. salt	2 T. saltpeter
2 lbs. sugar	4 qt. warm water

Place the meat in a crock or keg in alternate layers with the salt, ending with the salt. Let stand overnight or at least 12 hours. Dissolve the sugar, soda and saltpeter in warm water; let stand overnight also. In the morning, pour liquid over meat and let stand 4 days. On the fifth day, drain off liquid. Do not discard brine. Strain off the blood from meat and replace meat in the crock. Bring brine to boil and again pour over meat. Cover tightly by placing a cloth over top, then a board on top of cloth and a rock on the board. Let stand for 1 week before using. If meat is too salty for you, then parboil it, drain and then use.

Cured Meat

4 lbs. salt	50 lbs. beef
4 gal. water	Powdered Borax

Make brine of salt and water. Pour over the beef and weight it down. Let stand 4 days. Pour brine off, let get cold, put back on beef and leave it on 17 more days. It takes 3 weeks to take salt. Hang it up and smoke it ½ day, then dust it over with powdered Borax and hang away and it will keep for years. If it molds, wash it off before you cut it; it does not hurt it any. If you want to use the beef right away, you can hang it by the stove to dry.

MORMON TRAIL MINCEMEAT

2½ lbs. beef
2½ lbs. pork
1 lb. suet
Apples
2 lbs. raisins

5 T. cinnamon
3 T. allspice
2 leaves cloves
1 c. vinegar
2 c. water

Cook all meat and suet. If meat is quite lean, cook all together. (Cook until done.) Add an equal amount of apples as there is meat. Grind the apples and meat together. To this, add raisins, cinnamon, spices and vinegar. Cook in large kettle, covered, until apples and raisins are done. You may need to add water as it cooks.

BLAZING SADDLES DEER MINCEMEAT

3 pt. cooked meat
9 pt. apples
1½ c. raisins
1 pt. vinegar
1 pt. molasses
3 pt. sugar

3 tsp. cinnamon
3 tsp. ground cloves
2 tsp. nutmeg
6 tsp. salt
1 lb. margarine

Grind meat, apples and raisins. Place all ingredients in large cooking pot; cover. Cook over low heat until apples are transparent. Put in jars and seal.

OLD-FASHIONED CRACKLINGS & LARD

On hog killing day, the meat was ground, and the fat trimmings and skins were cooked for lard and cracklings. A fire was built outside under a large black wash kettle. A small amount of grease was added to get the meat cooking. A wooden paddle was used to keep the meat from sticking. Once it started cooking, the fire was increased and a watchful eye was necessary to prevent scorching. A few sticks of sassafras were used to help with the smell. The pork was cooked until cracklings were crisp. The lard was drained through a clean white cloth into a lard stand and stored in a cool place. The cracklings were used for other eating and cooking.

OKRA

Slice okra. Put on a piece of metal which has been covered with brown paper or on a white cloth to keep the okra off the metal or tin sheet being used. Place thinly on the sheet and put out in the sun. Cover at night. Let dry until ready to take off the paper. Remove and put in cloth bag until desired to use for cooking.

TO KEEP CORN FOR THE WINTER

When boiled, cut the corn off the cob and spread it on dishes; set these in the oven to dry. If you have no oven, it can be dried in a stove of moderate heat or round a fire. When perfectly dry, tie it up in muslin bags and hang them in a dry place. When you use it, boil it until soft in water; mix flour, milk, butter, pepper and salt together and stir in.

Tomahawk Hominy

The pioneers used wood ashes to make hominy, a trick they learned from the Indians. Remove husks; wash and shell the field corn to equal 1 quart. Add 2 quarts of cold water and 2 tablespoons of baking soda; soak overnight. In the morning, bring the corn and the soaking liquid to a boil in a kettle. Cook for 3 hours or until the hulls loosen. Add more water, if necessary. Drain off the water; wash corn in cold water, rubbing vigorously until the hulls are removed. Bring the corn to a boil again with 2 quarts of cold water; drain. Repeat the boiling step with fresh water; drain and add salt. Hominy was served with butter or gravy. Some cooks fried hominy in a skillet with bacon drippings. Hominy was frequently served as a cereal or as a vegetable.

Sun-dried Corn

Corn was cut as if it were going to be cooked, twice around the cob, and then spread out in the sun in a piece of tin.

Dried Pumpkin

Slice the pumpkin around in circles, take the seeds out, peel it and hang it on a stick crosswise of the joists of the house. Let it hang there until it dries. Store it in sacks. When ready to use, cook it several hours and season it with hog meat and grease.

SANDHILLS SWEET POTATOES

Boil potatoes until done. Slip off the skins and slice. Put on a clean, white cloth and put out in the sun each day. Then stack for winter use in pudding, pie, etc. or just peel and slice without boiling and set out to dry.

LEATHER BRITCHES BEANS

Wash and drain a batch of firm green beans. Remove ends and strings. Use large darning needle with heavy white thread and pierce the pod near the middle of each, pushing them along with thread so that they are about ¼ inch apart. Hang up the strings of beans in a warm, well-ventilated place to dry. They will shrivel and turn greenish gray. To cook in the winter time, as the pioneers did, cover with water and soak overnight. Drain, renew water and parboil slowly for ½ hour. Drain again. Cook slowly with ham hock or salt pork until tender.

Emigrant Sauerkraut

The cabbage must be firm. Trim, pick over, wash and shred it fine with a very sharp knife. The stalk should not be used. Line the bottom and sides of a barrel, keg or crock with cabbage leaves and put into it a layer of the cabbage three or four inches deep. Pound this down well with a wooden pounder, then sprinkle over it a small handful of salt, preferably table salt, then cabbage, then pound, then salt and so on, until four layers are put in. Cover the cabbage with a board cut to fit loosely on the inside of the barrel. Pound hard on the board until the cabbage is a compact mass. Take off the board and repeat the process until the barrel is full. Cover it with cabbage leaves, then a piece of clean cloth; on the cloth lay the board and on this put a heavy weight to keep down the mass. Set it away in a cool, dry place to ferment. As soon as the sauerkraut commences to effervesce, the covering of leaves should be thrown away, the scum removed, the kraut re-covered with a clean cloth, the board and weight thoroughly washed and replaced. As perfect cleanliness is necessary for its preservation, this process should be frequently repeated during the winter. It is ready for use in 20 or 25 days. It may be eaten raw or boiled with or without pork or bacon.

Onion Ropes

Leave onions out to dry, then braid tops of them into small rope and hang for winter. These were about 4 to 5 feet long "ropes of onions."

Dried Fruit

Dry fruit in the sun eight or nine days until done. Keep flies and bugs away. No need to turn. Hang big sacks of dried fruit in attic from the rafters.

OLD-KETTLE SULFURED APPLES

1 lg. tub
Brown paper
Sand

Hot coals
3 gal. cored apples
1 T. sulfur

Line a canner or large tub with brown paper. In the middle of the tub, place an old kettle or tin can containing a thick layer of sand or soil. On this layer of sand, place glowing red coals. Pour about 3 gallons of cored and quartered apples around the container of the coals and pour 1 heaping tablespoonful of sulfur on the coals. Cover the top of the tub with another layer of paper. Over the paper, place an old thick rug or folded blanket. Leave covered for several hours or overnight. These sulfured apples can be placed in a crock jar or in an old sheet or pillow case and left to dry. They can later be used for sauce or pies.

ON-THE-TRAIL APPLES

Wash, peel and core apples; slice very thin. Place in a single layer on a wire screen or white cloth and place in sun to dry. Take in at night. Apples will dry in 3 to 4 days of sunshine.

PRESERVED WILD PLUMS

Gather plums when fully ripe. Put in barrels, jars, tubs or anything else that will hold water; cover them with water after filling up. A scum will form on the top of the water which keeps them from the air. They need no careful sealing, only a safe place to keep from freezing during the winter.

Sun-dried Fruits & Vegetables

Pare and slice apples, apricots, peaches, pears, carrots, zucchini, celery, etc. Using a large blunt-nosed needle and heavy thread, pierce and string each piece of fruit or vegetable, leaving space for air to circulate between pieces. Hang out to dry in a partially sunny spot (direct sunlight may cause apricots to become bitter) or hang the strings across an open window that gets some sun. Fruits and vegetables dried this way will keep for months in an airtight container.

Conestoga Currant Jelly

Strip the currants off the stem and bruise them thoroughly. Put on the fire to heat and when at boiling point, strain them. To a pint of juice, allow a pound of loaf sugar. When the mixture begins to boil again, let it boil just 15 minutes.

Easy Plum Jelly

Plums   **Sugar**
Water

Cover plums barely with water and cook until soft. Strain juice through jelly bag or thin white cloth. For each cup of juice, add 1 cup sugar and bring to boil. Boil rapidly to jelly stage.

Apple Butter

1 gal. apple pulp   **1⅓ c. vinegar (or less)**
½ gal. sugar   **4 tsp. cinnamon**

Cook the pulp, then add sugar, vinegar and cinnamon. Cook until clear.

Pioneer Wild Plum Butter

Wash fruit and cook with water barely covering the fruit. When tender, press through a colander to remove seeds. Using equal amounts of fruit pulp and sugar, cook until it begins to thicken. In pioneer days before sealing wax was available, women put the butter into gallon stone jars, layed a piece of brown paper over the top and sprinkled sugar around the edges to seal.

Iowa Corn Cob Syrup

Cover 1 dozen large, clean red cobs with water. Boil 1 to 2 hours. Drain off the water and strain it. There should be a pint. Add two pounds of brown sugar to this and boil to desired thickness.

Heavenly Butter

Properly scald churn and pour thickened cream into it. Push dasher up and down until soft globules of butter are formed. Carefully lift these globules out into a large wooden bowl and work with a flat wooden paddle until all the buttermilk is removed. Add 2 teaspoons of salt for each pound of butter.

Rise & Shine Yeast

Boil 6 large potatoes in 3 pints of water. Tie a handful of hops in a small muslin bag and boil with the potatoes. When thoroughly cooked, drain the water on enough flour to make a thin batter. Scald it enough to cook the flour (this makes the yeast keep longer). Remove it from the fire and when cool enough, add the potatoes (mashed), also half a cup of sugar, 2 tablespoons of salt and a teacupful of yeast. Let it stand in a warm place until it has thoroughly raised, then put it in a cool place. The jug should be scalded before putting in the yeast. Two-thirds of a coffee cupful of this yeast will make four loaves.

Rendering Lard

Take the fat from the inside of a bacon hog, cut it small and put it in an iron kettle, which must be perfectly free from any musty taste. Set it over a steady moderate fire until nothing but scraps remain of the meat. The heat must be kept up, but gentle, that it may not burn the lard. Spread a coarse cloth in a wire sieve and strain the liquid into tin basins which will hold two or three quarts; squeeze out all the fat from the scraps. When the lard in the pans is cold, press a piece of muslin close upon it, trim it off the edge of the pan and keep it in a cool place. It may be kept in wooden kegs with close covers.

BRIGHAM BULGUR

Wash wheat in cold water and discard water. Cover the wheat with a generous amount of water and steam until water is absorbed and wheat is tender. This usually takes from 35 to 40 minutes. Spread the cooked wheat thinly on baking sheets and dry at 200° in a warm oven. Wheat must be very dry so that it will crack easily. When wheat is thoroughly dry, remove the chaff by rubbing kernels between the hands. A little moisture added either to the hands or to the surface of the wheat will assist in the removal of the chaff. Crack wheat in grinder to moderately fine. This processed bulgur is easily stored and may be used in many recipes. To store, place in a cool, dry, well-ventilated place. Do not store in airtight container. When properly stored, bulgur will retain its high quality for 3 to 4 months.

SUMMER SUN-DRIED HERBS

Cut herbs on a bright day just before they blossom. Tie in bunches; label and hang in a dry, airy, dustless place to dry as quickly as possible. When leaves are dry enough to crumble, strip from branches and place in fruit jars. Cover and label jars. Watch for a few days and if moisture forms on glass, remove leaves and dry longer.

Cooking on the Trail

"Echo Canyon"

Courtesy of Scotts Bluff National Monument

COOKING ON THE TRAIL

Perseverance and tenacity were the essence of the Mormon pioneer woman. Rain or shine, twice each day she started her campfire and baked, cooked, roasted and broiled enough food to satisfy whomever was under her care.

During the years on the Mormon Trail, the cooks managed to feed their people on little more than the bare necessities. Gravy and sourdough were the food staples of the Mormon pioneers. Nearly all the travelers' meals could be prepared using the bake oven, and gravy was always made to complement what was cooked. Gravy served as added nutrition, but mostly it served as a filler when other food was not available. Sourdough was so precious to the pioneer cook, she often slept with her sourdough starter so the yeast action would not be killed by the cold.

The pioneers used what food they found along the trail, and discovered that many items that otherwise seemed inedible became tasty on an empty stomach. Wild game, fish, turtles, fruits and wild vegetables were usually available throughout the spring and summer months. The supplies they brought along served them well, but for a healthy diet, wild food was essential.

The majority of the pioneers traveled in the spring and summer and did not encounter food shortages. However, the people who stayed through the first winter on the Trail at Winter Quarters suffered through the long, harsh Nebraska season with very little food other than what they had brought along. The pioneers ate a "nauseating" diet of corn bread, salt bacon, and milk for weeks on end, and lost nearly 600 people because of the meager food rations.

In later years, the pioneers planted crops in the spring upon leaving their wintering grounds. These crops fed those who would come in the fall to stay the winter.

Even through the hard times, the pioneers maintained hope for a good life in their new land. Following Brigham Young's encouragement to keep their fine things instead of trading them for food, the pioneers made willow baskets and washboards for trade, preserving their finery for their new life in the Salt Lake Valley.

Cooking on the Trail

Hit-the-Trail Salted Beef

Place meat in a pot of cold water and boil quickly. As soon as the water boils, take out meat and the water. Place with fresh, cold water; boil it according to quality and size of pieces, until thoroughly cooked.

Cooked Salt Beef

Wash beef well before cooking. When practicable, soak in cold water for 24 hours, changing the water 3 times. Cook as desired.

Exodus Fried Salt Pork

Cut the pork into thin slices; soak it in cold water 1 hour or longer. Drain and wipe dry. Have the frying pan very hot and dry. Put the sliced pork into the pan and fry brown on both sides. Season with pepper and serve. Previous to frying, the pork may be dipped into grated bread crumbs or rolled cracker. In this case, the pan should be greased.

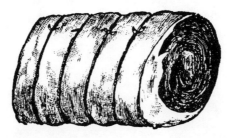

PAWNEE PEMMICAN

Combine equal parts of buffalo suet, dried fruit such as cherries, berries, plums and dried venison or other game. Add salt, if available, and pound the mixture in a bowl or a hollow rock, then form into bricks. Dry in the sun or near the fire in rainy weather. Pemmican may be eaten as is by biting off chunks, or bricks may be simmered in water to make a thick soup or stew.

MOUNTAIN MAIN BUFFALO JERKY

Slice buffalo meat along the grain into strips ⅛ inch thick, ½ inch wide and 2 to 3 inches long. Hang them on a rack in a pan. Bake at 200° until dry. To prepare outside, suspend them over a fire or drape them on bushes to dry in the sun.

TRAIL JERKY

1 (6-qt.) kettle   **Prepared strips of meat**
Salt (enough to float a raw
  egg)

Fill large kettle with water; add salt. Bring to a boil. Drop prepared meat in one piece at a time. Boil 3 minutes (10 to 12 at one time). Remove, drain and hang to dry. If flies or yellow jackets are a problem, add 1 tablespoon of black pepper to salt water.

GREAT PLAINS GAME STEW

Fill a large pot with small pieces of buffalo, deer, elk, antelope, bear meat or a combination of any of these. Cover with cold water and set over a fire. When partially cooked, you may add pieces of small game, such as rabbit, grouse, prairie chicken or salt pork. Continue to cook. After a time, add onion and any vegetables, such as carrots, potatoes, or turnips that you may have on hand. Cook until meat and vegetables are desired tenderness. Best served with sourdough biscuits for sopping up juice.

CAMPFIRE BUFFALO STEAK

Render some fat in a hot skillet. Add sirloin or buffalo steak and sear on both sides. At lower heat, cook as beefsteak until done. For gravy, add a tablespoon of flour to the pan drippings and cook until brown. Stirring constantly, add a cup of milk or water and bring to a boil. Salt to taste.

VENISON STEAKS

Select tender steaks from young animals. Cut 1 to 1½ inches thick. Broil close to source of heat, about 5 to 7 minutes per side or to desired degree of doneness.

KETTLE-FRIED VENISON HEART

1 venison heart   **Eggs**
Bacon fat

Squeeze heart in several waters to remove blood. Remove outer skin and membranes. Chop very fine and dry in bacon fat. Add eggs and scramble. Great for breakfast.

BREADED DEER STEAK

1 c. flour   **1 egg**
½ tsp. salt   **1 c. milk**
¼ tsp. pepper   **Deer steak**

Mix flour, salt and pepper in a bowl. Mix egg and milk in bowl. Pound meat with a meat hammer. Dip meat in egg mixture, then dip in flour mixture. Fry in skillet in lard until brown on both sides.

LIVER, ONION & BACON BAKE

Grease a baking pan. Place floured liver slices in pan. Slice onions to cover top of liver. Put bacon slices on top of onions. Cook until bacon looks done.

64

Mountain Stream Fried Fish

Small fish should be fried whole. Large fish should be cut up. Clean and wipe the fish dry. Rub it over with dry, sifted flour or dip it into well-beaten egg and then into bread crumbs or rolled cracker. Melt in a frying pan enough lard to well-cover the fish. When this is hot, put in the fish and fry both sides a clear golden brown. Just as the fish is turning brown, sprinkle it lightly with pepper and salt.

Smoked Fish

Fish
1 gal. water
Canning salt
2 tsp. molasses

¾ c. brown sugar
1 tsp. salt

Catch and clean fish by removing fish head and guts; leave scales on fish. In 1 gallon of water, add enough canning salt to float an egg. Add molasses, sugar and salt, and put in crock jar or large glass container. Soak fish for 24 hours. Remove fish and smoke until done.

Lone Prairie Quail On Biscuits

Split cleaned and dressed quail down the back and spread out flat. Sprinkle with salt and pepper. Brown in cast-iron skillet on both sides in lard. Add about ½ cup water. Cover and simmer 45 minutes to 1 hour until tender. Thicken broth with a little flour dissolved in water. Salt and pepper to taste. Spoon gravy over quail and serve over biscuits.

Braised Plains Partridges

4 partridges
Salt & pepper
¼ c. flour
¼ c. bacon drippings

½ c. chopped onion
1 c. chicken broth or water
¼ c. cream

Sprinkle partridges inside and out with salt and pepper; roll in flour. Heat bacon dippings in skillet. Add partridges and brown on all sides. Add onion, broth and cream; bring to a boil. Cover and cook over low heat 30 minutes or until tender.

Rifle Fried Rabbit

Unless the rabbit is tender, it is not suitable for frying. Prepare and clean the rabbit. Cut into pieces, wash and dip each piece into beaten egg; roll in cracker crumbs. Melt in a frying pan enough lard or beef drippings to cover the bottom of the pan, about a quarter-inch deep. Add rabbit, seasoning with salt and pepper and fry brown on both sides.

Settler's Stewed Rabbit

1 rabbit
Sm. onion
½ lb. pork

Salt
Pepper

Prepare and clean the rabbit and cut into pieces. Wash it again in cold water. Mince the onions. Cleanse pork and cut into small pieces. Put the rabbit into a pot with a little over a pint of cold water. Add onion, pork, salt and pepper; cover and simmer until tender, stirring occasionally.

SIOUX FRIED FROGS LEGS

¾ c. fat
2 eggs, well beaten
1 tsp. salt
½ tsp. pepper

1 c. yellow cornmeal
1¼ c. water
3 lbs. frogs legs

Heat fat in a deep skillet over medium-high heat. In a wide, shallow bowl combine eggs, salt, pepper, cornmeal and water. Dip frog legs in batter, making sure they are well coated. Fry in fat about 30 minutes, turning occasionally until legs are golden brown and firm to the touch.

PLATTE RIVER TURTLE STEW

2 lbs. turtle meat
2 bay leaves
1 c. celery
1 onion
1 T. parsley
Pepper

2 tsp. salt
2 T. flour
3 T. chicken fat or lard
Water
2 T. vinegar
Flour
½ c. condensed milk

Combine in kettle. Cut up turtle meat (snapping turtle is the best), bay leaves, celery, onion, parsley, pepper to taste, salt, flour and chicken fat or lard. Add water to barely cover and boil until tender. You may have to add water before meat is tender. When tender, add vinegar. Make a paste of flour and water. Add to stew. Gradually add condensed milk. Stir in liquid and boil another 3 to 5 minutes.

CAMPFIRE BOILED BEANS

2 lbs. beans (great northern or
  navy)
1 T. baking soda

Water (to cover)
Diced bacon, ham or hocks

Soak beans overnight, making sure there is at least 1½ inches or more of water over the beans. In the morning cook, making sure there is enough water to cover the beans. Bring to a boil. Pull away from heat and simmer ½ hour. Add baking soda and stir briskly; drain and rinse with cold water. Return beans to kettle; cover with water (1½ inches) as before and place over fire, adding any of the following: diced bacon ends, ham (cut in ½-inch cubes), or ham ends or hocks. Ham bones can also be used. After bringing to a boil, pull away from heat and let cook slowly for 3 hours or more, making sure they are covered with water.

CHIMNEY ROCK BAKED BEANS

1 qt. beans
Water
1 sm. onion
Pinch salt

1 spoonful sugar
1½ spoonfuls molasses
Sm. piece bacon or side pork

Soak beans in water to cover overnight; drain. Add remaining ingredients and cook two to three hours.

Dusty Trail Bean Soup

1 pt. beans	1 T. butter
2 qt. water	Salt & pepper to taste

Soak the beans overnight in cold water. Next morning, drain and add 2 quarts of water. Cook the beans slowly for three hours, stirring frequently. When they are soft, add butter, salt and pepper. Cook 10 minutes longer and serve.

Fried Potatoes With Salt Pork

1 c. diced salt pork	5 potatoes, pared & sliced
1 med. onion, coarsely chopped	¼ tsp. pepper

Fry salt pork in a large, heavy skillet about 10 minutes, stirring occasionally. Add onion and cook until tender. Add potatoes and cook over moderate heat until potatoes are done, stirring occasionally. Sprinkle with pepper.

Fried Raw Prairie Potatoes

Wash, pare and slice the potatoes very thin. They will hold the shape better if cut lengthwise. Have brisk but not a fierce fire. Melt in a frying pan enough lard to float the potatoes. When lard is boiling hot, drop in the sliced potatoes, a few at a time, so as not to chill the fat. Fry to a light brown; turn if necessary. Salt as desired.

BURNT BROWN GRAVY

2 T. bacon fat
4 T. flour

1 c. water

Put fat in small frying pan over medium-high heat. Add flour. Stir with fork until mixture is a deep brown. Add water, while stirring. Stir until gravy is smooth. Serve over hot biscuits.

FRIED SALT PORK & GRAVY

Good piece salt pork
1 beaten egg

Flour to coat pork

Gravy:

Equal amounts of flour and
  grease

Pepper
Milk

Slice pork thin. Dip slices of pork in egg, then in flour. Fry in enough hot lard to coat fry pan. Fry until crisp. Remove pork and scrape leavings from frying pan. Add equal amounts of flour and grease to frying pan. Heat until bubbling. Add pepper to taste. Pour in milk gradually, while stirring constantly, using 1 cup of milk to each table-spoon of flour and grease.

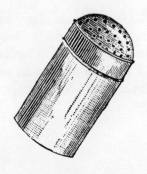

WILD COUNTRY BACON GRAVY

⅓ lb. bacon
½ c. flour
1 c. water

Salt to taste
Milk

Fry bacon until crisp. Remove from skillet. Dissolve flour in water and salt. Pour into skillet with drippings from bacon. As mixture boils and thickens, add milk until desired gravy consistency. Serve over biscuits.

SUNRISE SAUSAGE GRAVY

1 lb. sausage
2 or 3 T. flour

2 c. milk
2 c. water

Brown sausage; drain. Add flour and cook with sausage until brown. Add milk and water. Cook on medium heat, stirring frequently, until thickened. Serve with biscuits.

SCOUTS FRIED CAKES

Combine 1½ cups of flour with 1 cup of water; mix well with a fork. Using plenty of flour on hands and a breadboard, roll out dough to a thickness of ¼ inch. Cut into 2-inch squares. Render beef fat in a skillet and add squares of dough. Brown slowly on both sides. Sprinkle with salt to taste. Makes about 20 cakes.

SAGEBRUSH SODA BREAD

To make dough, mix 1 teaspoon baking soda with 1 cup warm water. Add 2¼ cups flour and 1 teaspoon of salt. Knead well. The dough may be used at once or allowed to rise overnight in a warm place. In either case, flatten dough to a thickness of 1 inch. Place on a greased skillet and bake at 400° for about 25 minutes.

SOUTH PASS SOURDOUGH BREAD

Sourdough bread was used by pioneers when baking powder or yeast were not available. They carried with their camp outfit, a one-half gallon crock with a lid that fitted securely down into the mouth of the crock. When camp was pitched and a big fire built, they would get out the crock, also a pan half-full of flour, make a hole in the center of the flour and into it, pour the sourdough from the crock. Then add soda and a little salt, according to their judgment. The amount of soda was determined by the sourness of the batter. The flour was then mixed in to make a soft dough. This was flattened into a flapjack shape, placed in a hot bake-skillet and covered with a lid that had been heated on the coals. Then some red-hot coals or bits of burning wood were placed under the skillet, and some on top of the lid to keep it at baking temperature. When the bread was nice and brown, it was cooked through. The sourdough batter was made originally by mixing flour, a small amount of salt with enough warm water to make a batter thick enough to bask a spoon, placing the crock in the warm earth near enough to the fire to keep it warm. When it began to ferment and bubble, it was set aside. When sufficiently sour, it was used in the bread. Each time a start was left in the crock, more flour and water were added and it was placed in a warm place. In this way, it would be sufficiently sour to be used for the next meal.

HUNGRY MAN'S CORNMEAL BATTER CAKES

1 qt. sour milk
1 tsp. soda in enough hot
  water to dissolve it

2 tsp. salt
2 eggs, beaten
Cornmeal, sifted

Mix all ingredients and add enough sifted cornmeal to make a thin batter. Cook on a griddle, over a quick, clear fire. Each cake should be buttered as soon as cooked and kept hot until served.

MEAGER MILK SOUP

1 egg
Piece of butter (size of an egg)
3 heaping T. flour

A pinch of soda
3 pt. boiling milk
Salt & pepper

Place egg, butter, flour and soda in a bowl; stir into a stiff dough. Chop with a knife into tiny pieces. Stir into boiling milk seasoned with pepper and salt. Boil a minute or two.

HANDCART HARDTACK

4 c. flour
4 tsp. salt

Water

Mix flour and salt together in bowl. Add just enough water (less than two cups) to make the mixture stick together. Roll the dough out to ½ inch thick and shape it into a round rectangle. Cut into squares about 3 x 3 inches. After cutting, use a nail to punch four rows of four holes each in each 3 x 3-inch piece. Then flip each piece over and punch through again. Place on an ungreased cookie sheet and bake at 375° for 30 minutes. Turn each piece over and bake for another 30 minutes. The tack should be slightly brown on both sides.

Pioneer Pudding (Sop)

Break up dried bread into a bowl. Pour boiling water over it and then drain off excess water. Add sugar and cream. Serve while hot.

Lumpy Dick

Bring one quart of milk to a boil in a skillet and sprinkle white flour a little at a time slowly, not stirring but gradually "poking" and mixing so it will not get slick and smooth, but ever so slightly lumpy. Keep at high heat, but do not boil hard for about fifteen minutes. Use enough flour so that it has a fairly thick consistency (like cereal). Serve warm with very thick cream. To use as pudding, add butter, sugar and cinnamon or nutmeg. Use as a morning breakfast and served with butter and salt. Another way to make Lumpy Dick is to slowly add white flour to boiling water until it reaches the consistency of mush. Add a pinch of salt and serve, either hot or cold, with milk and sugar.

Mormon Trail Johnny Cake

2 c. cornmeal
1½ tsp. salt

2 tsp. sugar (opt.)
2½ c. boiling water

Combine cornmeal, salt and sugar, if desired. Stir in water until mixture forms a thick batter. Drop by tablespoon onto a well-greased griddle and flatten to about ½ inch thick. Cook until golden brown, turning once. Yield: About 18 cakes.

SOURDOUGH GRIDDLE CAKES

2 c. sourdough starter
5 c. flour
4 c. warm water
2 eggs
4 T. oil

½ c. condensed milk
4 T. sugar
1 tsp. salt
2 tsp. baking soda

Mix starter, flour and warm water the night before. Reserve 2 to 3 cups to replenish starter. To the remaining mixture, add eggs, oil and milk; mix well. In a separate bowl. Add sugar, salt and soda. Sprinkle over dough and gently fold in. Let rise 3 to 4 minutes. Fry on hot griddle. Serve immediately.

MITCHELL PASS MUSH

No one ever "took sick" from eating mush and milk or fried mush in any suitable quantity. "Mush and milk" is seldom relished because few people know how to make the mush. The whole secret is in cooking it thoroughly. Rightly made, it is not "hasty pudding." A well-made "mush" is one that has boiled not less than a full hour. Two hours are better. The meal needs to be cooked, then it is both good and palatable. The rule is: mix it very thin and boil it down, avoiding any burning or scorching, and salt it just right to suit the general taste. Prepare a good kettle full for supper, to be eaten with milk, sugar, molasses, syrup, sweetened cream or sweetened milk. If a good supply is left to cook, and cut in slices and fried well in the morning, the plate of wheaten bread will be little in demand. It must be fried well, not crisped or burned or soaked in fat. If thoroughly soaked through in the kettle, it will only need to be heated through on the griddle. If not cooked well in the kettle, longer frying will be necessary.

CIRCLING-UP DOUGHNUTS

Mix three eggs, two cupfuls of sugar, one and one-half cupfuls of milk, butter the size of a small egg, two teaspoonfuls cream of tartar rubbed into a quart of flour, one teaspoon soda dissolved in milk, a little salt and one-half nutmeg. Use enough flour to roll out soft; cut in fancy shapes and drop into boiling lard. A slice of raw potato put in the fat will prevent it from burning.

STEWED DRIED APPLES

Pick over the apples carefully, then wash them in cold water; drain. Soak overnight in enough cold water to cover. Put apples and water in which they have been soaked, into a pot (iron should not be used; an earthenware well glazed crock or stone jar is preferable); cover closely and simmer until they are tender.

BAKED EARTH DRIED APPLE PIE

Soak 2 cups of dried apples in water overnight. Drain off water and mix apples with ½ cup sugar and 1 teaspoon each of allspice and cinnamon. Line an 8-inch pan with a crust. Add the apple mixture. Dot with 3 tablespoons of butter and cover with a second crust. Make a few slashes in the top for ventilation and bake at 350° for about 1 hour or until the crust is golden brown.

SUNDOWN BREAD PUDDING

1 c. sugar
1½ tsp. cinnamon
2 T. flour

2½ c. water
1 c. day-old bread, broken

Mix sugar, cinnamon, flour and ½ cup water together. Boil 2 cups water. Slowly stir in the mixture; cook until thick. Add 1 cup broken day-old bread. Cool.

EGGLESS, MILKLESS, BUTTERLESS CAKE

1 c. brown sugar
1¼ c. water
1 c. raisins
⅓ c. lard
½ tsp. salt

1 tsp. nutmeg
1 tsp. cinnamon
2 c. flour
4 tsp. baking powder
¾ c. chopped nuts

Boil sugar, water, raisins, lard, salt and spices for 3 minutes. When cooked, add flour and baking powder; mix well. Add nuts. Bake in a one-loaf bread pan in moderate oven for 45 minutes.

ASH HOLLOW ARROWROOT

Use milk or water as preferred. Put a heaping teaspoonful ground arrowroot into a cup and mix with a little cold milk. Stir into a pan containing a pint of either cream or water that has been brought to a boil, adding a little salt. Let it simmer a few minutes and then pour out. May be sweetened or flavored with grated nutmeg as desired; should be made only as it is wanted.

Utopia –
End of the Trail

"Salt Lake Valley"

UTOPIA – END OF THE TRAIL

"The first duty of a saint when he comes to this
valley, is to learn how to grow a vegetable; after
which he must learn how to rear pigs and fowl, to
irrigate his land, and to build his house. The rest
will come in time."

~ Brigham Young

After enduring the journey where fresh food was a rarity, the pioneers
made it their goal to fill every stomach full of fresh, well-prepared food.
They planted gardens, raised animals and grew crops. Each year saw
more and more land under cultivation, providing plenty of food for the
newly arrived emigrants.

The pioneers arrived in the Salt Lake Valley with little but their own
dignity and ingenuity. These became their means for success in this new
land. The Mormons initiated the first irrigation in Utah by white men.
This allowed their fruits and vegetables to grow in abundance.

Along with their success at raising fruits and vegetables, the pioneers
fulfilled their plan of raising excellent livestock. The few cows, pigs,
sheep and chickens that had traveled the trail became the seedstock for
great herds.

During the first few years, the Mormon women cooked outdoors using
bake ovens or iron kettles. They had no control over the weather; they
learned to make the best with what they had and took advantage of every
cooking opportunity. For this, their training on the trail served them well.
They used the precious few cooking utensils they had managed to bring
with them. Items such as milk pans, brass buckets and iron pots had
served them well during the journey, and continued to for years until the
Mormons could trade or buy from other settlers traveling west.

Not only were new cooking utensils scarce, many spices and sugars the
pioneers were accustomed to could not be found or grown in the Salt
Lake Valley. Again, the pioneers improvised, using nutmeg, molasses,
and honey for sweetening. Because of this talent and perseverance, it was
not long before the Mormon women became known as the best cooks in
the West.

Utopia - End of the Trail

BREADS

Winter Quarter's Wheat Bread

5 to 5½ c. flour
1 T. active dry yeast
1¾ c. water

1 tsp. salt
⅓ c. packed brown sugar
3 T. butter

Combine 2 cups of flour and the yeast. In a separate pan, heat and stir brown sugar, shortening, 1¾ cups water and 1 teaspoon salt until warm and butter almost melts. Add to flour mixture; beat. Using a spoon, stir in as much remaining flour as you can. Turn out onto a lightly floured surface. Knead in enough remaining flour to make a moderately stiff dough that is smooth and elastic (6 to 8 minutes total). Shape into a ball. Place in a lightly greased bowl; turn once. Cover; let rise in a warm place until doubled (1 to 1½ hours). Punch dough down. Turn out onto a lightly floured surface. Divide in half. Cover and let rest 10 minutes. Lightly grease two loaf pans. Shape each half of dough into a loaf. Place in pans. Cover; let rise in a warm place until nearly double (45 to 60 minutes). Bake at 375° for 40 to 45 minutes or until done. Remove from pans; cool. Makes 2 loaves.

Tin Cup Soda Biscuits

3 c. flour
1 tsp. salt
1 tsp. sugar

1 tsp. baking soda
3 T. shortening
2 c. milk

Sift together the flour, salt, sugar and soda. Cut in the shortening, using two knives or fingers. Slowly add the milk until a soft dough is formed. Roll out mixture on a floured board and cut with a biscuit cutter. Bake in a very hot oven at 425° for 15 minutes.

Thanksgiving Pumpkin Bread

2 c. flour
1 c. packed brown sugar
1 T. baking powder
1 tsp. ground cinnamon
¼ tsp. salt
¼ tsp. baking soda
¼ tsp. ground nutmeg
⅛ tsp. ground ginger or
  ground cloves

1 c. pumpkin
½ c. milk
2 eggs
⅓ c. butter
½ c. chopped walnuts
½ c. raisins

In a large bowl combine 1 cup of the flour, the brown sugar, baking powder, cinnamon, salt, baking soda, nutmeg and ginger or cloves. Add pumpkin, milk, eggs and butter. Beat for 2 minutes. Add remaining flour; beat well. Stir in nuts and raisins. Pour batter into a greased loaf pan. Bake at 350° for 60 to 65 minutes. Cool for 10 minutes on a wire rack. Remove from the pan; cool thoroughly on a wire rack. Wrap and store overnight before slicing. Makes 1 loaf.

JAIL ROCK JOHNNY CAKE

2 eggs, beaten
2 c. buttermilk
2 T. molasses or honey
2 c. cornmeal

½ c. flour
1 tsp. soda
1 tsp. salt
2 T. butter

Beat eggs until light. Add buttermilk, molasses or honey. Combine dry ingredients and stir into batter. Add butter. Pour into buttered pan and bake at 425° for about 20 minutes or until done. Cut into large squares. Makes about 24 pieces.

RISE-N-SHINE CORNMEAL MUSH

3 c. water
1 c. cornmeal

1 tsp. salt

Bring water to a boil in a heavy pan. Stir cornmeal into 1 cup cold water, then add to boiling, salted water. Cook slowly and stir often for about 1 hour. Pour into a small loaf pan to cool. In the morning, slice and sprinkle with flour and fry, golden brown on both sides. Serve with butter and syrup.

CRACKLING CORNBREAD

1 c. finely diced fresh pork fat
1 c. flour
1 c. cornmeal
1 c. buttermilk

2 beaten eggs
1 tsp. baking soda
¾ tsp. salt
1 T. sugar

Cook pork fat until crisp. Drain and reserve drippings and crackling. Add flour to drippings. Blend until smooth. Add cornmeal, buttermilk, eggs, soda, salt, sugar and crackling. Pour into greased iron skillet. Bake in hot oven (425°) for 15 to 20 minutes.

Trailside Fried Bread

Make a pan full of risen bread dough. After dough rises, take sharp knife and pull up dough with other hand about size of large plum. Heat a pan about ½ full of lard to medium-high temperature. Drop bread dough into lard. Will float on one side when nice and brown; turn over and brown other side. Put on towel; serve warm. Great for breakfast. We eat them for every meal until dough is gone.

Old-fashioned Noodles

Put about 1 quart or a sifter full of flour in a bowl. Put in some salt, then about 4 or 5 egg yolks. Do not use the whites as they make the dough hard to roll. Instead of whites, put half of an egg shell of cold water for each egg you use. Mix as you would pie dough, adding in flour if needed. Then divide in about 3 pieces, roll out thin and let dry. Turn them once in a while until they are dry enough so they will not stick. Then roll up and cut fine. Do not let them get too dry or they break.

Gobbled Up Dumplings

1 beaten egg
½ c. milk
Pinch of salt

1 tsp. baking powder
Flour

Combine egg, milk, salt and baking powder. Add enough flour to make a stiff batter. Let this stand for 1 hour before cooking. Drop by spoonfuls into boiling broth. Cover tightly and boil for 10 minutes. Serve at once.

DAYBREAK DROP DOUGHNUTS

2 eggs
½ c. milk
¼ c. shortening
½ c. sugar

1 tsp. nutmeg
2 c. flour
1 T. baking powder

Heat a large amount of shortening in frying pan. Mix together eggs, milk and shortening. Add sugar, nutmeg, flour and baking powder. When well mixed, drop by teaspoon into hot grease. Fry until brown, turning over once. Remove from grease and roll in sugar or cinnamon.

FT. LARAMIE FRIED CAKES

½ c. sugar
1 c. sweet cream
Butter
2 eggs

Pinch of salt
1 tsp. soda
Flour

Mix sugar, sweet cream, a piece of butter the size of a walnut, eggs, pinch of salt, soda and enough flour to make a stiff dough. Roll out about twice as thick as pie dough and cut in strips ¾ inch wide and 8 inches long. From the center, wrap the one strip around the other and pinch together. Drop one by one into boiling lard.

HOMEMADE SODA CRACKERS

4 c. flour
½ tsp. baking soda
1 tsp. salt

¾ c. sour milk
1 c. butter

In large mixing bowl sift in dry ingredients; mix well. Add milk and butter; stir to a stiff dough. Roll and turn over repeatedly, until dough becomes very stiff. Roll out very thin and cut into squares. Prick with a fork and bake at 400° until edges are brown.

GARDEN GROVE GRAHAM CRACKERS

3 c. whole-wheat flour
½ tsp. salt
½ tsp. baking powder

¼ tsp. cinnamon
6 T. butter
½ c. honey

Sift together flour, salt, baking powder and cinnamon into a bowl. Melt together butter and honey. Pour this into the dry ingredients. Mix with a fork, then mush dough together with your hands. Do not overmix. Place on a lightly greased cookie sheet, rolling it to ⅛-inch thickness. Cut rectangles with a knife and prick with a fork. Bake 10 minutes in a moderate oven (375°).

SIDE DISHES

SIMPLE SMOOTH MASHED POTATOES

6 med. potatoes   Butter
Water   Milk
2 T. salt

Peel potatoes and rinse. Slice potatoes in about ¼-inch slices. Do not dice or quarter potatoes. Slicing will insure a smoother consistency. Put potatoes in pot; cover with water and add salt before cooking. Boil until done; drain. Add butter and about ⅓ cup milk. Mash or whip until light and fluffy.

HOME-CUT FRIED POTATOES

6 to 8 potatoes   Hot grease
Water   Salt to taste

Peel potatoes and cut as thin as possible. On a medium potato you should get about 20 slices. Let sit in water for a few minutes. Many of the potatoes will curl when they soak in water a while. Fry in hot grease, stirring often. Potatoes should turn out crisp. Salt as preferred.

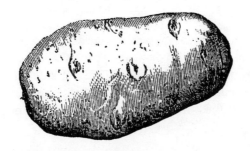

OLD-TIMERS FRIED PARSNIPS

Boil the parsnips until tender; scrape off the skin and cut lengthwise into slices a quarter of an inch thick. Dip each slice into beaten egg or flour. Put into a frying pan enough lard or beef-dripping that when melted will just cover the bottom of the pan. When this becomes hot, put in the parsnips and fry until brown on both sides. When cooked, take them up, drain off the grease; season with pepper and serve. They may be fried without the egg or flour.

SMITHS SUCCOTASH

2 T. butter
2 c. cooked lima beans
2 c. whole-kernel corn
1 tsp. salt

¼ tsp. pepper
1 tsp. sugar
¾ c. light cream

Melt butter in a saucepan. Stir in beans, corn, salt, pepper, sugar and cream. Heat 5 minutes over low heat. Yield: 6 servings.

HARVEST DAY ACORN SQUASH

1 acorn squash
⅓ c. butter

¼ c. brown sugar
½ tsp. salt

Cut squash in half lengthwise; remove seeds and stringy fibers. Place cut side down in baking dish or shallow pan in ½ inch hot water. Bake at 350°, uncovered, for 30 minutes. Turn cut side up and drain off water. Combine butter, brown sugar and salt. Spoon evenly into centers of squash halves. Bake for 15 minutes, basting once or twice.

DELICIOUS FRIED CABBAGE

1 sm. head cabbage   1 med. onion
½ lb. bacon   Salt & pepper to taste

Slice cabbage into 4 quarters. Slice thin. Cook bacon until crispy, leaving a small amount of grease in pan. Slice onion. Combine bacon, cut into pieces, with diced onion and cabbage. Add salt and pepper to taste. Simmer in large fry pan over low heat; cook until tender.

SUNDOWN CORN PUDDING

6 ears fresh corn   ½ c. cream
½ c. butter   2 eggs, well beaten
¼ c. sugar   1½ tsp. baking powder
1 T. flour   Salt to taste

Scrape uncooked corn from the cob. Heat butter until melted. Stir in sugar and flour; remove from the heat. Gradually stir in cream. Add well-beaten eggs, baking powder and salt; mix well. Fold in corn. Stir until well mixed. Grease a baking pan. Pour in corn mixture. Bake 45 minutes at 350°.

CUMBERLAND FRIED CORN

8 tender ears corn   1 tsp. black pepper
2 T. sugar   1 to 2 c. cold water
1 T. salt   2 T. butter
1 T. flour

Cut corn from cob. Combine sugar, salt, flour and pepper and add to corn, mixing well. Add water. Melt butter in skillet over medium to low heat. Add corn mixture, cooking slowly until creamy, about 30 minutes. Stir continuously. Remove from heat.

FIRESIDE BOILED GREEN CORN

Corn for boiling should be full grown, but young and tender. Sweet corn is the most desirable. When the grains become hard, it is too old for boiling. Test by piercing the grain; the milk should escape in a jet. Clean by stripping off the outer layer of shucks, turn back the inner shucks, pick off the silk, bring back the inner shucks over the grains, tie the ends. This process preserves the sweetness of the corn. Put the corn into a pot of boiling salt water, enough to cover it. Cover and boil long enough to cook. Any exposure to heat after this injures the corn. When cooked, cut off the stalk close to the cob and remove the shucks. Cold boiled corn may be cut from the cob and fried, or fried mixed with mashed potato. Green corn may be cooked in the shuck in hot ashes for about one hour.

FT. BRIDGER FRIED BEANS

Boil and drain beans. Put just enough butter or beef-dripping into a frying pan that when melted will just cover the bottom of the pan. When this becomes hot, put in the beans and fry brown; stir them occasionally so that they will brown uniformly.

88

BLAZING BAKED BEANS

1 qt. navy beans
½ lb. salt pork
1 tsp. salt

3 T. molasses
2 T. sugar
1 c. hot water

Pick over beans; wash and cover with cold water. Soak overnight. Drain; cover with fresh water. Cook slowly until skins burst. Drain beans. Cut rind of pork every ½ inch. Put beans in pot, covering pork, leaving rind exposed. Mix salt, molasses and sugar. Pour over beans. Add water to cover beans. Cover bean pot. Bake 6 or 8 hours in a slow oven (250°). Uncover last hour of cooking so the rind may become brown and crisp. Add water as needed.

COMPANY COLESLAW

2 eggs
1 c. sugar
1 c. vinegar

1 T. butter
Cabbage, shredded

Beat eggs, then add sugar, vinegar and butter. Cook and stir until thickened; cool. Pour over shredded cabbage.

WILTED LETTUCE

Place in a vegetable dish lettuce and dandelions picked and washed. Cut across the dish four or five times and sprinkle with salt. Fry a small piece of fat ham or bacon until brown; cut into small pieces. When very hot, add a cup of vinegar and pour it boiling hot over the greens. Be sure to have the fat so hot that when the vinegar is poured in, it will boil immediately. Add half a cup or a cup of vinegar according to the strength of vinegar and quantity of lettuce. Mix it well with a fork and garnish with slices of hard-boiled eggs.

Soddy Spiced Beets

1 gal. beets, cooked & sliced	2 T. cinnamon bark
2 pt. vinegar	1 T. whole cloves
2½ c. brown sugar	

Mix beets and vinegar. If too sour, vinegar can be weakened with water. Then add sugar and spices. Place in stone jar, tie shut and keep in a cool cellar. These will keep a year and can be opened from time to time as used.

Old-time Baked Turnip

1 turnip (2 to 3 lbs.)	2 T. brown sugar
Water	2 T. molasses
Salt to taste	2 T. dark syrup
1 egg	Butter
¼ c. milk (scant)	Nutmeg

Peel turnip and cut in about 1-inch chunks. Wash and place in pot with water to cover. Add salt to taste; cook until tender. Drain; add egg and milk which have been beaten together. Mash all together and add sugar, molasses and syrup; blend well. Pile lightly in buttered dish. Dot with butter and sprinkle top with nutmeg. Bake at 350° for 30 to 45 minutes or until top is lightly browned. Very good with any kind of meat, fish or poultry.

MAIN DISHES

ROUND-UP BAKED CHICKEN

¾ c. flour
1½ tsp. salt
¼ tsp. pepper
½ tsp. dried sage

2 chickens, cut in serving
  pieces
½ c. shortening
½ c. chopped onion
2 c. cream

Combine flour, salt, pepper and sage. Roll chicken pieces in mixture. Heat shortening in skillet. Add chicken pieces and brown on both sides. Place in a large shallow baking pan. Add onion to skillet and cook until tender. Remove and add to chicken; drain fat from skillet. Add a small amount of boiling water; stir to scrape up brown bits. Pour over chicken with cream. Bake at 350°, uncovered, for 1 hour.

HIGH NOON ROAST GOOSE

1 dressed goose
Salt
½ gal. dry bread cubes
Salt & pepper to taste

Sage, to taste
Milk
Water

The goose may be cleaned 2 to 3 days ahead of time, placed in a roaster and placed outside to freeze. The night before it is to be used, bring indoors for thawing. Remove most of the fat; rub both inside and outside with salt. Boil gizzard, heart and liver until tender. Grind and return to broth in which it has been cooked. Combine with dry bread cubes, salt, pepper and sage for stuffing with enough milk to moisten. Stuff goose and place in roaster, adding 1 pint of water. Add a little more water as needed to keep from getting dry. Baste occasionally. Bake 3 hours or more in a hot oven (425°).

Chicken Pot Pie

1 chicken
1 egg
1 c. sweet milk (the richer the
 better)

½ c. butter
Flour

Cut up and cook chicken making broth. Mix together egg, milk and butter; add enough flour to make a stiff dough. Roll this very thin and cut in small squares. Drop in the broth and let boil 10 minutes.

Utah Chicken & Dressing

1 hen, cooked
1 tsp. salt
3 qt. water
1¼ c. chopped onion
1¼ c. chopped celery
3 qt. crumbled cornbread

1 qt. white bread crumbs
1 tsp. pepper
Sage, if desired
4 eggs

Cook hen in 3 quarts water with salt. Boil with onions and celery until falling off bones; debone. Pour hot broth and chicken with onions and celery over bread crumbs. Add pepper and sage, if desired. Beat eggs and add to mixture. Pour in greased dish. Bake at 350° for 45 minutes or until done.

WAGON-HO FRIED CHICKEN

3 eggs, beaten
½ c. milk
Salt
Pepper

12 pieces chicken
1½ c. flour
⅔ skillet of shortening

Beat eggs by hand. Add milk to eggs and beat again. Salt and pepper chicken well. Dip chicken in egg mixture and dredge in flour. Shake off excess flour. Place in hot skillet of shortening. Brown on one side on medium heat. Then turn on the other side until golden brown. Drain pieces on paper towels.

WESTERN CHICKEN WITH DUMPLINGS

1 qt. water
2 tsp. salt
2 carrots, peeled & sliced
1 onion, sliced

1 branch celery
1 stewing chicken, cut into
  pieces
1 c. milk
⅓ c. flour

Heat water to boiling. Add salt, carrots, onions, celery and chicken. Cover and simmer (don't boil) for 2½ to 3 hours, or until chicken is tender. Remove chicken from broth and keep warm. Strain broth and measure; add enough water to make 3 cups. Return broth to sauce pan and heat. Put milk and flour in jar with a cover and shake until mixture is smooth. Cook about 5 minutes; add chicken to gravy. Make dumplings and add to simmering chicken about 20 minutes before serving.

Dumplings:

2 c. flour
3 tsp. baking powder
1 tsp. salt

¼ c. shortening
1 c. milk

Sift together flour, baking powder and salt. Cut in shortening until mixture looks like coarse cornmeal. With fork, mix in milk to make a soft dough; stir as little as possible. Drop by spoonfuls onto chicken pieces. Simmer 20 minutes longer. Serve at once.

STUFFED GOOSE NECKS

Goose meat, uncooked
Bread stuffing
Goose neck skins (whole)

1 onion, sliced
1 c. hot water

Grind scraps of goose meat finely and mix with the stuffing. Tie one end of the neck skin tight with clean string and stuff with mixture. Tie second end, place in baking pan, add onion and water and bake at 350° until brown and crisp, basting occasionally. Slice and serve hot.

94

Iron Skillet Gravy

4 T. butter or bacon grease   1½ tin c. of milk
3 or 4 T. flour

Put the butter or bacon grease in the skillet. Add flour to make a paste.
Keep stirring until a nice brown color. Add milk and continue stirring
until desired thickness.

Cowboy Cream Gravy

¼ c. pan drippings   ½ tsp. salt
¼ c. flour   ¼ tsp. pepper
2½ to 3 c. hot milk

Pour off all except ¼ cup drippings from skillet in which meat was
fried. Place skillet over medium heat. Add flour; stir until browned.
Gradually add hot milk. Cook, stirring constantly, until thickened and
bubbly. Stir in salt and pepper. Serve hot.

Mormon Pot Roast Of Beef

¼ c. flour
2 tsp. salt
½ tsp. pepper
1 (4 to 5-lb.) boneless beef
  shoulder pot roast
1 T. shortening
½ c. water

3 med. potatoes, pared & cut
  into ½-in. cubed
2 c. diced carrots
2 c. (½-in.) cubes rutabaga or
  yellow turnips
1 c. chopped onion

Mix flour, salt and pepper; rub over beef roast. Heat shortening in 12-inch skillet or Dutch oven until hot; brown beef on all sides. Drain fat from skillet; add water. Heat to boiling. Reduce heat. Cover tightly and simmer for 2 hours. Arrange vegetables around beef. Add ¼ cup water, if necessary. Cover and simmer, stirring vegetables occasionally, until beef and vegetables are tender, about 45 minutes. Remove beef and vegetables from skillet. Serve broth with beef. Yields 12 servings.

Scotts Bluff Swiss Steak

Shortening
3½ lbs. of 1½-in. pot roast
  (round bone type)
3 c. chopped tomatoes
3 onions

2 cloves garlic
3 green peppers, diced
Salt & pepper to taste
2 tsp. paprika
1 c. water

Put shortening in Dutch oven and brown the meat, adding the liquid from the tomatoes. Simmer for 10 minutes. Peel and quarter the onions. Add onions, chopped garlic cloves, diced green peppers, salt and pepper and paprika. Place tomatoes on top of meat. Add water. Cover: cook until brown over slow heat, about 2 hours. Serve rice on the side or mashed potatoes.

WAGON MASTER BOILED DINNER

3 to 4-lb. corned beef brisket
Water
8 sm. onions
8 med. carrots

4 potatoes, quartered
2 turnips, cubed
1 med. cabbage, cut into
   wedges
Caraway seed

Place brisket in large pot. Cover with cold water; cover tightly; simmer 3½ hours. Add onions, carrots, potatoes and turnips. Sprinkle with caraway seed. Cover; simmer 20 minutes. Remove meat to warm platter. Add cabbage to liquid and simmer, uncovered, 10 to 15 minutes longer.

TRAIL'S END CHOPPED BEEF HASH

3 c. leftover steak, roast, etc.
4 med. onions, chopped
3 med. raw potatoes, peeled &
  cubed

3 T. butter
3 c. stock or leftover gravy
Salt & pepper to taste

Melt butter. Add onions and meat. Cook 5 minutes, but do not let onions burn. Add potatoes, stock (or gravy), salt and pepper. Simmer until gravy is thick and potatoes done (25 to 30 minutes). Serve on split buttered hot biscuits, if desired.

"One man killed a very large tortoise and divided it to five or six families and only kept one meal for themselves. It was fine, it was the only one I ever tasted." ~ *Elizabeth Lamb*

Trading Post Brown Stew

2 T. fat
2 lbs. boneless stew beef
Salt & pepper to taste
Flour

Water
6 potatoes
6 onions
6 carrots

Place fat in pot or Dutch oven and heat. Season meat with salt and pepper and flour well. Brown well in fat. Cover with water and simmer slowly until almost tender. Add vegetables and cook until tender.

Salt Lake Glazed Ham

1 (16 to 20-lb.) ham,
  precooked
1 lb. brown sugar
2 T. dry mustard

6 T. honey
1 tsp. black pepper
1 c. water

Combine brown sugar, dry mustard, honey and black pepper. Coat ham with portion of mixture and place in roaster with 1 cup water. Cover; bake 4 to 5 hours at 350°, basting with remaining mixture every hour.

Nauvoo Pork Chops & Apples

6 pork chops
Fat
3 or 4 unpeeled apples,
  cored & sliced

¼ c. brown sugar
½ tsp. cinnamon
2 T. butter

Brown chops on both sides in hot fat. Place apples in greased baking dish; sprinkle with sugar and cinnamon. Dot with butter; top with chops. Cover. Bake at 350° for 1 hour and 30 minutes.

FORT LARAMIE PORK CHOPS

8 pork chops
Fat
6 med. potatoes, thick sliced
2 med. onions, quartered

2 c. cracker crumbs, seasoned
to taste with salt, pepper & 1
garlic clove, chopped

Use a Dutch oven preheated with ¼ inch of fat. Coat pork chops with crumbs and brown on each side. Move pork chops to one side of the Dutch oven and stack, if necessary. Place potatoes and onions in remaining side of oven; cover and cook about 45 minutes with less coals on the bottom and more coals on the lid. Check meat after the first 15 to 20 minutes for burning while turning meat and potatoes and adjusting the amount of coals as necessary. Turn lid and oven periodically about ¼ turn in opposite directions to prevent burning of food on top and bottom.

SAINT'S SAUERKRAUT & PORK HOCKS

4 to 5 lbs. smoked pork hocks
4 to 5 c. water
1 onion, sliced

½ tsp. marjoram or leaves
2 lbs. sauerkraut, drained
½ tsp. celery seed (opt.)

Place meat, water, onion and marjoram in Dutch oven. Heat to boiling. Reduce heat; cover tightly and simmer 1 hour or more. Remove oven from heat. Drain liquid, being sure to reserve 1 cup. Add sauerkraut, celery seed and reserved liquid to meat. Cover and simmer 30 more minutes.

Lone Tree Lamb Chops

Dust the lamb chops with flour, salt and pepper. Brown quickly on both sides in savory drippings. Place in baking dish. Scrape and slice carrots. Peel several small onions and arrange the vegetables around the lamb chops. Sprinkle with salt and pepper. Add one cup of water. Cover and bake in the oven one-half hour.

To Fry & Broil Fish Properly

After cleaning fish, lay them on a folded towel. When wiped dry, roll in wheat flour, rolled crackers, grated stale bread or Indian meal, whichever may be preferred. Wheat flour will generally be liked. Have a thick-bottomed frying pan or spider with plenty of sweet lard, salted - a tablespoon of salt to each pound of lard - for fresh fish which have not been previously salted; let it become boiling hot, then add fish and let fry gently until one side is delicate brown; turn. When both are done, remove carefully and serve quickly, or keep covered with a tin cover and set dish where it will stay hot.

Rocky Mountain Baked Fish

½ c. sliced onion
¼ c. butter
¾ tsp. salt
Black pepper to taste
1½ c. soft bread crumbs

White perch, yellow perch, large-mouth bass, striped bass, flounder or other fish fillets
¾ c. milk

Saute onions in butter until lightly browned. Season with salt and pepper. Add bread crumbs. Arrange fillets in baking dish. Spoon crumb mixture on top of fillets. Pour milk around fillets. Bake at 350° for 45 minutes. Bottom of baking dish can be lined with soft bread slices.

Sweet Water Salmon
With Creamed Peas

2 c. cooked salmon
1 c. mashed potatoes
½ tsp. salt
Little pepper

1 c. bread crumbs
1 egg, slightly beaten
1 T. melted butter
2 c. peas, cooked

White Sauce:

2 T. butter
2 T. flour

2 c. milk
½ tsp. salt

Mix salmon with mashed potatoes, salt and pepper. Form into croquettes. Roll in bread crumbs, then egg and then crumbs again. Fry in hot butter. **White Sauce:** Melt butter in pan; add flour. Stir until hot and foamy but not brown. Add milk and cook, stirring constantly, until thickened. Add salt. Add 2 cups cooked peas. Pour over salmon croquettes.

Country-fried Venison

2 lbs. venison steaks
2 c. flour
2 T. salt

2 T. pepper
½ c. bacon grease

Tenderize steaks with meat mallet. Combine flour, salt and pepper. Dredge steak through flour mixture. Be sure to fill each cranny with flour. Fry in grease until each side is golden brown.

Musket Shot Pickled Deer Heart

Deer heart   Vinegar
Pickling spice

Slice heart in half and boil until done. Take off stove; drain and cool.
Cut up bite size, removing any gristle. Put ½ teaspoon pickling spice
on bottom and top of jar. Fill with meat and cover with vinegar; seal.

Stew Pot Pigeons

Gizzards & livers (pigeons)   6 pigeons
Grated ham (amount you   Water
  wish)   Butter
2 c. bread crumbs   Flour
Herbs (your choice amount)   1 med. onion
6 hard-boiled egg yolks

Stew the gizzards and livers until tender. Chop livers fine and mix
with grated ham, bread crumbs and herbs. Make into a force meat,
rolling it around the egg yolk and stuff in pigeons. Place birds in a
stew pan with water and a little butter. Make gravy of the gizzards
chopped fine, flour and onion. Pour over pigeons. Stew gently until
done.

*"Our supply was flour, meal, beans, dried bread, crackers, dried
apples, sugar and milk, with some butter and bacon and a few
dried parsnips. No wonder we were glad to get something out of
a garden."*
                                        ~ Elizabeth Lamb

Wilderness Quail With Gravy

8 quail, dressed
½ tsp. salt
¼ tsp. pepper
¼ c. butter

1 c. chicken broth
2 T. flour
2 T. water

Sprinkle quail with salt and pepper. Brown quail on both sides in butter in a large skillet. Cover with chicken broth and simmer 40 minutes or until tender. Remove quail from skillet; set aside. Measure pan drippings. Add water, if necessary, to measure 1 cup. Combine flour and 2 tablespoons water. Gradually add pan drippings. Cook over low heat, stirring constantly, until thickened and bubbly. Return quail to skillet; heat thoroughly. Remove quail to a serving platter and serve with gravy.

DESSERTS

Old-Fashioned Bread Pudding

2 c. sifted flour
½ tsp. salt
4 tsp. baking powder

4 T. shortening
¾ c. milk

Mix dry ingredients in a mixing bowl. Add shortening, mixing in with fingers. Add milk to make a soft dough, handling lightly. Roll or pat out dough to make oblong shapes ½ inch thick. Spread generously with jam of any kind. Roll as for jellyroll. Place in pan. Cover tightly and steam 30 minutes or more. Cut in serving slices and serve with cream or favorite sauce. Place a cloth in the bottom of the pan to prevent the pudding from becoming water-soaked.

Heavenly Rice Pudding

6 c. milk	3 egg yolks
¾ c. rice	2 tsp. vanilla
1 c. cream	¼ tsp. salt
¾ c. sugar	1 tsp. cinnamon

Rinse pan with cold water and pour in milk. Bring just to a boil. Stir in rice and reduce heat to simmer. Cook 1 hour, stirring occasionally. Mix in cream, sugar, egg yolk, vanilla and salt. Sprinkle with cinnamon upon serving.

Indian Blackberry Dumplings

Part 1:

3 pt. ripe blackberries	1 c. sugar
¾ c. water	2 T. butter

Combine and let set.

Part 2: (Dumpling Batter)

2 c. flour	1 tsp. salt
3 T. sugar	1 egg
3½ tsp. baking powder	Milk

Sift dry ingredients into bowl. Add eggs and mix. Add enough milk to make a stiff batter. Bring Part 1 to a boil. Drop dumpling batter, a spoonful at a time, into boiling mixture. Cover and cook for 15 to 20 minutes. Serve with cream.

SUET PUDDING

1 c. milk
1 c. raisins
1 c. molasses
½ tsp. cinnamon
1 c. chopped suet

2 c. flour
1 tsp. soda
¼ tsp. nutmeg
¼ tsp. cloves
¼ tsp. allspice

Mix all ingredients together and put into greased pudding mold. Steam
3 hours in a covered kettle.

SPOTTED DICK

⅓ c. flour
Pinch of salt
⅓ tsp. baking powder
⅓ c. fresh bread crumbs

⅓ c. shredded suet
¼ c. sugar
¾ c. currants (raisins)
4 to 6 T. milk

Half fill a steamer with water; put on to boil. Mix together flour, salt,
baking powder, bread crumbs, suet, sugar and currants in a bowl. Make
a well in the center; add enough milk to make a fairly soft dough.
Form into a roll on a well-floured board. Wrap loosely in a greased
cloth, tying both ends. Steam over rapidly boiling water for 1½ to 2
hours. Unwrap the pudding. Put in a hot dish and serve with custard
or with a sweet white sauce flavored with cinnamon.

Pioneer Bread Pudding

2 c. cubed bread
2 c. milk
3 T. butter
¼ c. sugar

2 eggs
1 tsp. vanilla
Sprinkle of cinnamon

Place bread into buttered baking dish. Scald milk. Add butter and sugar. Beat eggs slightly. Add to milk mixture. Add vanilla. Pour over bread and sprinkle with cinnamon. Bake at 350° for about 1 hour.

Indian Boiled Pudding

1 tsp. saleratus
1½ c. sour milk
2 eggs, well beaten

Cornmeal
1 c. dried cherries

Dissolve saleratus in milk. Mix in eggs. Sift in dry cornmeal until it is the consistency for thick griddle cakes. Stir in dried cherries. Put in bag and boil for one hour. **Pudding Sauce:** Sweeten cream and flavor with nutmeg. Pour over pudding.

Timeless Egg Custard

4 eggs
1 c. sugar
1 T. flour
1 c. sweet milk

1 tsp. vanilla
4 T. butter, melted
1 unbaked pie shell
Nutmeg

Beat eggs and sugar. Add flour, milk, vanilla and butter. Pour into unbaked pie shell. Sprinkle nutmeg on top. Bake at 300° until light brown.

WESTWARD APPLE CORNMEAL PUDDING

12 apples
1 qt. sifted cornmeal
1 qt. new milk
Salt
4 spoonfuls chopped suet

1 teacup good molasses
1 tsp. soda, dissolved in water
Sugar
Cream

Pare and core apples; slice them very thin. Then stir cornmeal into new milk; add a little salt. Next add the apples, chopped suet and molasses, then the soda dissolved in a little water. Mix all together well. Pour into a buttered dish and bake 4 hours at 350°. Serve hot with sugar and cream.

VALLEY MOLASSES CAKE

½ c. butter
½ c. sugar
1 c. molasses
2 eggs
3 c. flour
1 tsp. cinnamon

1 tsp. ginger
1 tsp. cloves
2 tsp. baking soda
1 c. boiling water
Nuts
Raisins

Cream butter and sugar. Add molasses. Add eggs. Combine flour, cinnamon, ginger and cloves. Dissolve soda in water. Alternately add flour mixture and water to batter. Mix well. Add nuts and/or raisins, if desired. Bake at 375° for 45 minutes.

Apple Brown Betty

4 slices bread, toasted
3 c. sliced peeled baking
  apples
½ c. sugar
½ c. packed brown sugar

1 tsp. ground cinnamon
¼ c. butter, melted
½ c. cream

Tear toast into bite-sized pieces. Place in a greased casserole dish. Top with apples. Combine sugars and cinnamon; sprinkle over apple. Drizzle with butter. Cover and bake at 350° for 1 hour, stirring after 30 minutes. Serve warm with cream.

Miraculous Blackberry Cobbler

2 c. sugar
⅓ c. butter
2 c. flour
2 tsp. baking powder

1 tsp. salt
1 c. milk
2 c. blackberries
2 c. boiling water

Cream 1 cup sugar with butter. Add flour, baking powder, salt and milk; mix well. Pour into baking pan. Pour blackberries over batter. Sprinkle remaining sugar over blackberries. Pour boiling water over top. Bake at 350° for 50 minutes or until golden brown. Serve plain or with cream.

Rally Cry Vinegar Pie

1 c. water
1 c. sugar
½ c. flour

3 T. vinegar
Salt & nutmeg
Butter (size of an egg)

Stir all together and boil. When thick, pour into baked pie shell. Serve with whipped cream.

OLD-FASHIONED CREAM PIE

1 unbaked pie crust
3 heaping T. flour (4 if a deep
  crust)
¾ c. sugar

Pinch of salt
Butter size of walnut
Milk

Measure all ingredients except milk. Mix together with fingers. Pour in pie crust and fill with milk. Bake 1 hour and 15 minutes at 350°.

RIPE GRAPE PIE

2½ c. grape pulp & skins
¾ c. sugar

2 T. flour
3 T. melted butter

Wash fully ripened grapes. Separate pulp and skins. Cook pulp slowly until soft. Rub through sieve. Combine sieved pulp and skins. Combine sugar and flour. Add to grape mixture. Add butter. Pour into pastry-lined pan. Cover with top crust or with strips of pastry. Bake at 425° for about 25 minutes.

PRAYER CIRCLE SWEET POTATO PIES

½ c. butter
1 c. mashed sweet potatoes
2 c. sugar
1 c. cream
1 tsp. vanilla

1 tsp. nutmeg
1 tsp. cinnamon
3 T. flour
3 beaten eggs
2 pie shells

Melt butter and add to sweet potatoes; mix. Add sugar, cream, vanilla, nutmeg, cinnamon, flour and beaten eggs. Divide evenly into 2 pie shells. Bake.

OLD-FASHIONED APPLE PIE

2 pie crusts
2 T. flour
1 c. sugar

Apples (fresh)
Cinnamon
Butter

Prepare pastry for double-crust pie and roll out. Combine flour and sugar; sprinkle ¼ cup into bottom of crust. Add enough apples (peeled and sliced) to fill shell. Add remaining sugar/flour mixture. Sprinkle generously with cinnamon and dot with butter. Make a few small cuts in top crust (to allow steam to escape) and put over fruit. Bake at 450° for 35 to 40 minutes or until apples are tender.

GENOA GOOSEBERRY PIE

Top and tail the gooseberries. For one quart of gooseberries, line two deep pie dishes with plain pastry. Fill with the berries. Add nearly 1 cup of sugar to each pie. Cover with an upper crust and bake in a quick oven for 40 minutes. For ripe gooseberry pie, use one-third less sugar.

NEVER-FAIL PIE CRUST

1 c. lard or shortening
3 c. sifted flour
1 egg

5 T. water
1 tsp. vinegar
1 tsp. salt

Cut lard into flour, leaving pea size lumps; set aside. Beat egg; add water, vinegar and salt. Stir in flour mixture, forming a ball. Cut in half and roll out. Handle as little as possible. Makes 2 crusts.

SUN-SCORCHED APPLE FRIED PIES

4 c. dried apples   ½ to ¾ c. sugar
2 c. water

Combine apples and water in large saucepan. Bring to a boil. Reduce
heat. Cover and simmer 30 minutes or until tender; cool. Mash slightly,
if necessary. Stir in sugar and set aside.

Pastry:

3 c. flour, sifted   1 egg, beaten
1 tsp. salt   ¼ c. water
¾ c. lard or shortening   1 tsp. vinegar

Mix all ingredients. Divide pastry into thirds. Roll each portion to
¼-inch thickness. Cut into 5-inch circles. Place about 2 tablespoons
apple mixture on half of each pastry circle. To seal, dip fingers in
water and moisten edges of circle. Fold in half, making sure edges are
even. Use fork and press pastry edges on both sides firmly together.
Heat ½ inch lard in large skillet. Cook until golden brown. Turn only
once. Drain on paper towels. Yields 1½ dozen pies.

STEWED DRIED APPLES, APRICOTS & PEACHES

Wash fruit thoroughly and soak overnight in the water (cold) they are
to be cooked in, using only enough water to cover them. Put the fruit
on the fire in a vessel, not iron (an earthenware stone jar, well glazed,
is very suitable), and simmer slowly (do not boil), closely covered, for
two hours. Do not stir to break the fruit, and thus render it unslightly.
When the fruit is cooked put in plenty of sugar; let it then cook five
minutes. If sugar is added before the fruit is cooked, it will harden.

OLD-FASHIONED GINGERBREAD

2½ c. flour
1½ tsp. soda
½ tsp. salt
1 tsp. cinnamon
½ tsp. cloves
1 tsp. ginger

½ c. shortening
½ c. sugar
1 egg
1 c. molasses
1 c. boiling water

Sift flour, soda, salt and spices together. Cream shortening, sugar, egg and molasses together. Mix dry ingredients and creamed mixture together, then stir in boiling water. Bake in moderate oven (350°) for 30 to 40 minutes.

FRIED APPLE FRITTER

Apples, grated
2 T. sugar
2 c. flour

3 eggs
1 c. milk
2 tsp. vanilla

Prepare apples and grate. Mix sugar, flour, eggs, milk and vanilla together. Add grated apples. Spoon into skillet and fry like a pancake.

MOLASSES SUGAR CELEBRATION COOKIES

¾ c. shortening
1 c. sugar
¼ c. molasses
1 egg
2 c. flour

2 tsp. baking soda
½ tsp. cloves
½ tsp. ginger
1 tsp. cinnamon
½ tsp. salt

Melt shortening over low heat. Remove from heat and allow to cool. Add sugar, molasses and egg; beat well. Sift together flour, soda, cloves, ginger, cinnamon and salt; add these to first mixture. Mix well and chill thoroughly. Form into 1-inch balls. Roll in granulated sugar. Place on greased cookie sheet 2 inches apart. Bake at 375° for 8 to 10 minutes.

ECHO CANYON CORNMEAL COOKIES

¾ c. butter
¾ c. sugar
1 egg
1½ c. flour
½ c. cornmeal

1 tsp. baking powder
¼ tsp. salt
1 tsp. vanilla
½ c. raisins, optional

Mix butter and sugar in a large bowl. Add egg; beat well. Add flour, cornmeal, baking powder, salt and vanilla; mix well. Add raisins, if desired. Drop dough from a teaspoon on a greased baking pan. Bake in moderate oven (350°) for about 15 minutes or until lightly browned.

"The first duty of a saint when he comes to this valley, is to learn how to grow a vegetable, after which he must learn how to rear pigs and fowl, to irrigate his land, and to build his house. The rest will come in time." ~ Brigham Young

Old-Fashioned Eggless Applesauce Cake

2 c. packed brown sugar
2 c. raisins
2½ c. dried apples, cooked &
    still warm (or warm
    applesauce)
1 c. butter

1 c. chopped nuts
3 tsp. baking soda
1 tsp. cinnamon
3 c. sifted all-purpose flour

Mix together brown sugar, raisins, applesauce, butter and nuts. Mix together soda, cinnamon and flour; add to brown sugar mixture. Pour batter into a greased and floured pan. Bake at 350° for 55 to 60 minutes or until cake tests done. Cool for 10 minutes and remove from pan.

Salt Lake Shortcake

2 c. flour
4 tsp. baking powder
3 T. sugar

1 tsp. salt
⅔ c. cream
⅓ c. milk

Combine flour, baking powder, sugar and salt. Add cream blended with milk; mix well. Put into buttered pan, preferably one round layer pan. Bake at 375° until browned. Split shortcake and cover with sweetened wild berries and thick cream.

Wagon Wheel Water Cake

½ c. butter
1 c. sugar
2 eggs
1 c. water

2 c. flour
1 tsp. soda
Flavor with nutmeg or lemon

Beat the butter, sugar and eggs to a cream, then add the other ingredients. Stir well and bake quick, 400° for 30-40 minutes.

UTOPIA GEM CAKE

2 eggs
Rich sweet cream
Butter

1 c. white sugar
1½ c. flour
2 tsp. baking powder

Break eggs into a cup and fill with cream. Add to this in a mixing bowl, a lump of butter the size of a walnut, sugar, flour and baking powder. Bake in gem pans or 2 layers, at 375° for 30-40 minutes.

MISSIONARY MOLASSES TAFFY

1 c. molasses
1 T. butter

1 T. vinegar
1 tsp. soda

Combine all ingredients and boil to hard ball stage. Remove from pan and let cool enough to pick up with hands. Pull until cold and yellow in color. Place in pan and cut in squares.

HONEY CANVAS CANDY

2 c. honey
1 c. sugar

1 c. cream

Combine all ingredients and cook slowly until it reaches the hard ball or crisp stage when tested in cold water. Pour out onto buttered platter. Cool until cool enough to handle. Grease hands and pull with fingertips until golden in color. Cut or break into pieces.

CHILDREN'S VINEGAR CANDY

2 c. white sugar　　　　　　**2 T. butter**
½ c. apple cider vinegar

Combine all ingredients and cook until mixture is brittle when dropped in cold water. Cook slowly so that it does not burn. When done, pour on a buttered plate. Mark into squares while warm and let set until cool and hard.

TRAIL RIDER CORN BALLS

2 c. molasses　　　　　　**Sprinkle of salt in molasses**
1 c. sugar　　　　　　　　**6 qt. popped corn**

Boil molasses, salt and sugar until it forms a soft ball in cold water. Pour over popped corn; mix well as syrup will go to the bottom. To keep hands from sticking to mixture, dip them in a pan of cold water. Make corn balls.

SNOW ICE CREAM

Fresh clean snow　　　　　**2 tsp. vanilla**
2 eggs　　　　　　　　　　**3 c. cream**
1 c. sugar

When it snows outside, gather a container of fresh, clean snow. Beat eggs well. Mix with sugar, vanilla and cream. Add snow to mixture, using enough snow to make it thick.

THIS & THAT

MORMON TEA

When the pioneers were directed to give up their cherished tea and coffee, they found several comforting substitutes - a cup of hot water with cream or milk and a little sugar or honey added.

SAGE TEA

Made by brewing the leaves of garden sage and seasoning with cream and sugar. Many mothers used catnip; the weed grew everywhere, to make tea for supper or breakfast as well as to give to babies when they had colic.

BARLEY COFFEE

Barley was browned in the oven, then ground to make a delicious coffee.

MORMON VALLEY TEA

Mountain Rush, from which a tea, commonly known as Brigham Tea or Mormon Valley Tea, was widely used by the pioneers. It was steeped like tea and taken with or without milk and sugar according to taste.

Harvest Day Drink

1⅓ c. molasses   ⅔ c. vinegar
2 tsp. ginger   7 pt. cold water

Mix ingredients together in order given. Serve on hot days. Makes 1 gallon. This drink was served on farms when harvesting was done. It's a real thirst quencher.

Wagon Train Pancake Syrup

1 c. water   1 lb. brown sugar

Just heat water to boiling. Lower heat; stir in sugar. Continue to stir over low heat until sugar is completely dissolved. Serve hot. Makes 1 pint.

Homemade Baking Powder

½ tsp. cream of tartar   ¼ tsp. cornstarch or
¼ tsp. baking soda   arrowroot powder

Mix together. Equals 1 teaspoon baking powder.

Homestead Bacon Dressing

4 slices bacon
½ c. sugar
½ tsp. salt
1 T. cornstarch

1 beaten egg
¼ c. vinegar
½ c. milk or cream

Fry bacon slowly. In a saucepan put sugar with salt and cornstarch; mix thoroughly. Add beaten egg and vinegar, mixing well again. Lastly, add milk or cream and bacon; let cool to desired thickness. Excellent on lettuce and spinach.

Boiled Salad Dressing

1 T. ground yellow mustard
½ tsp. ground turmeric
2 T. flour
1 tsp. salt
½ tsp. cayenne pepper

1 pt. vinegar
2 egg yolks
¾ c. sugar
4 T. oil

Mix dry ingredients, except sugar, in a bowl. Add gradually to this mixture a little cold vinegar, mixing it well to a creamy paste. Add the yolks of two eggs; beat again. Heat to boiling point: 1 pint good vinegar and sugar. Pour this in the mixture from the bowl, stirring briskly to keep it from being lumpy. Cook until thick and creamy. When done, set to one side and add oil. Stir until well mixed. Put in self-sealed can and keep in cool place until used up.

MAYONNAISE

½ c. sugar
1 T. flour
1 tsp. salt
1 tsp. prepared mustard

1 c. milk
½ c. vinegar
1 egg, beaten

Mix sugar, flour, salt and mustard together. Add milk. Blend well and last add vinegar and egg. Place over stove and cook until thick.

OLD-TIME METHOD OF MAKING COTTAGE CHEESE

Place milk in several pans to clabber. After clabbering, place in large, flat-bottomed kettle. Place the kettle on the stove on low heat and do not let the milk simmer or boil. While the milk is heating, slowly cut through the clabbered milk crosswise with a knife to separate the cords and let the milk heat evenly. When the curds of milk and whey have separated (the thin whey will come to the top), take a clean bag and pour mixture into it. When it is all in the bag, squeeze lightly, and hang on clothes line overnight. In the morning, add salt and enjoy.

New Recipes from Old Favorites

Courtesy of Scotts Bluff National Monument

"Mormon Party Near Fort Bridger"

NEW RECIPES FROM OLD FAVORITES

One hundred and fifty years have passed since the advent of the Mormon Trail. As times change, so do styles and techniques related to food preparation.

Cooks are using conventional ovens rather than Dutch ovens, are cooking indoors rather than exposed to the elements and are using modern-day refrigeration rather than cellars. Times have definitely changed, and cooking has changed with it.

> "... got breakfast, washed the dishes, made the bed
> and sewed a little on my garment. In the afternoon I
> baked a loaf of bread, cleaned a hog's face and put it
> to boil and made a pot pie for supper, then washed the
> dishes and spent the evening sewing."
>
> ~ Mary Richards,
> in her diary upon reaching
> the Salt Lake Valley

Although cooking techniques and daily activities have changed, traditional recipes remain important to modern-day Mormons. Recipes have been handed down through generations and have been changed to fit cooking standards of the time. Just as food was important to the pioneers for energy and nutrition, the same food is used today in remembrance of those who traveled the Mormon Trail, forging a new life for the people of the Mormon church.

The Mormon celebration of thanksgiving, called Harvest Day, is a day spent in thankful remembrance of those who forged this new life for the Mormon people. Harvest Day features a celebration of traditional food. Like the Pilgrims who suffered in the new land before they prospered, the Mormons faced hard times before their settlement thrived.

Many traditional recipes maintain important roles in holiday and celebration meals. Harvest Day, Christmas, New Year's Eve, New Year's Day, Pioneer Day and weddings, among other holidays, include modern-day versions of traditional recipes. Harvest Day may feature pumpkin bread, and Irish soda bread may be eaten on New Year's Eve. Food will forever play an important role in Mormon holiday celebrations.

New Recipes From Old Favorites

BREADS

Johnnycake

1¼ c. flour
¾ c. cornmeal
2 T. sugar
2 tsp. baking powder
½ tsp. salt

1 c. milk
¼ c. cooking oil
4 T. molasses
2 eggs

Preheat oven to 350°. Grease an 8 or 9-inch square pan. Combine flour, cornmeal, sugar, baking powder and salt. Stir in milk, oil, molasses and eggs, mixing until dry. Bake 20 to 25 minutes. Makes 1 loaf.

Sour Dough Rolls

2 c. self-rising flour
1½ sticks oleo

8 oz. sour cream

Spray muffin pan with cooking spray. Sift flour. Melt oleo and add to flour. Add sour cream to other ingredients. Stir until well blended. Spoon into muffin pan. Bake at 350° for 20 to 30 minutes.

FREEZER BISCUITS

2 c. flour
4 tsp. baking powder
½ tsp. cream of tartar
2 T. sugar

¼ tsp. salt
½ c. vegetable shortening
⅔ c. milk
1 egg, beaten

Mix together flour, baking powder, cream of tartar, sugar and salt. Cut in the shortening. Beat milk and egg together; add to mixture. Knead; roll out dough and cut biscuits. Freeze. Do not thaw before baking. Bake in 425° oven for about 20 minutes or until done.

EGG NOODLES

4 eggs
4 tsp. soft margarine
4 drops yellow food coloring

½ tsp. salt
3 c. flour

Beat eggs, margarine, food coloring and salt together. Add 3 cups flour and mix well with hands into smooth ball (may not need all of the flour). Divide dough into 2 sections. Slice dough into ½-inch slices. Flour slices lightly and let dry a few minutes. Put each slice through noodle machine 4 or 5 times. Flour and let dry a few minutes. Put slices through noodle slicer. Spread thinly on waxed paper; lightly flour. Let dry completely before bagging. This recipe will make approximately 6½ loose cups of noodles.

WHIPPED COUNTRY BUTTER

½ c. vegetable oil
1 lb. margarine

¾ c. buttermilk

Combine all ingredients in a mixing bowl; beat until well mixed. For a good old-fashioned taste, chill before serving.

SOUPS & STEWS

CHUCK WAGON STEW

1 tsp. sugar
¼ c. all-purpose flour
2 lbs. lean stew beef
2 T. melted shortening
2 tsp. salt
¼ tsp. pepper
1 tsp. chili powder
¼ tsp. thyme

1 bay leaf
2 tomatoes, peeled &
  quartered
1 (10½-oz.) can beef broth
6 sm. potatoes, cut up
6 sm. carrots, cut up
6 sm. onions
3 or 4 stalks celery, cut up
1 can peas

Combine sugar and flour. Coat beef with flour mixture and brown in hot shortening. Add seasonings, tomatoes and broth to meat; cover and simmer over low heat, about 1½ to 2 hours. Stir in vegetables except peas. Cover and cook another 30 minutes. Add peas; cover and cook 12 more minutes.

VENISON STEW

2 lbs. venison
1 env. onion soup mix
1 lg. can tomatoes
1 tsp. oregano
1 T. olive oil

1 T. meat tenderizer
2 T. white vinegar
2 bay leaves
Salt & pepper

Mix all ingredients in a pot. Let marinate for 1 hour or less, if needed, then cook. Simmer, covered, for 1 to 2 hours. Serve over rice. Great on a cold day!

Bean Soup

2 c. mixed dry beans
2 T. salt
2 T. baking soda
2 qt. water
2 c. cooked ham, cubed
1 bay leaf
½ tsp. basil
1 onion, chopped

2 carrots, chopped
2 stalks celery, chopped
2 T. lemon juice
½ to 1 tsp. chili powder
½ tsp. pepper
1 (28-oz.) can tomatoes
1 tsp. salt

Cover beans with water and add salt and soda. Cook until tender. Rinse.
Add 2 quarts water, ham, bay leaf and basil. Bring to boil and simmer
for 3 hours. Add onion, carrots, celery, lemon juice, chili powder,
pepper, tomatoes and salt. Cook until vegetables are tender.

Leek & Potato Soup

4 slices bacon, chopped
6 leeks, thinly sliced
¼ c. chopped onion
2 T. flour

4 c. chicken broth
6 lg. potatoes, thinly sliced
1 T. + 2 tsp. chopped fresh
  parsley
8-oz. carton sour cream

Cook bacon in a Dutch oven over medium heat for 5 minutes. Add
leeks and onion; saute 5 minutes. Reduce heat to low; add flour, stirring
until smooth. Cook 1 minute, stirring constantly. Gradually add broth;
cook over medium heat, stirring constantly, until thickened. Add potatoes and parsley; cover and simmer 45 minutes. Add sour cream, stirring
well; simmer for 10 minutes.

Salmon Chowder

½ c. chopped celery
½ c. chopped onion
½ c. chopped green pepper
1 clove garlic, minced
3 T. margarine
1 c. chopped potatoes
1 c. shredded carrots

2 c. chicken broth
1½ tsp. salt
½ tsp. pepper
½ tsp. dill weed
1 c. canned salmon
1 (17-oz.) can cream-style corn
1 (13-oz.) can evaporated milk

Saute celery, onion, green pepper and garlic in margarine in saucepan. Add potatoes, carrots, broth and seasonings. Simmer for 20 minutes. Stir in salmon, corn and evaporated milk. Simmer for 10 minutes or until heated through.

FISH

Grilled Salmon

1 med. green bell pepper
1 lg. onion
1 to 2 lbs. salmon (fresh or frozen)

Salt & pepper to taste
1 (16-oz.) bottle Italian dressing

Prepare pan out of double aluminum foil for grill. Cut pepper and onions into rings. Place salmon on foil; cover with onions and peppers. Season with salt and pepper. Pour Italian dressing over. Do not cover. Grill 1 hour, turning 3 to 4 times on low. Very good!

BAKED FISH

1 c. uncooked rice (white or
  wild)
1 stick real butter

1 pkg. white fish
1 can cream of mushroom
  soup

Cook rice and drain. Melt butter in oven-proof baking dish. Place fish
on top. Bake until fish is flaky. Mix rice and soup. Pour into baking
dish. Carefully place baked fish on top. Drizzle butter over all. Reheat,
if necessary. May use vegetarian soups for more color.

SALMON DILL LOAF

1 (15-oz.) can salmon
6-oz. can water chestnuts,
  drained & diced
1 beaten egg
½ c. diced celery
½ c. diced green onion
⅓ c. plus 2 tsp. ketchup

1 tsp. chopped fresh dill or ¼
  tsp. dry
¼ tsp. pepper
¼ tsp. Worcestershire sauce
Dash of Tabasco sauce (opt.)
Lemon or lime wedges

Combine salmon, water chestnuts, egg, celery, green onion, ketchup,
dill, pepper, Worcestershire sauce and Tabasco sauce. Spray loaf dish
with nonstick cooking spray. Turn salmon into loaf dish. Bake until
top of loaf is lightly browned, 35 to 45 minutes. Serve warm or cold
with lemon or lime wedges.

Almond Heaven Trout

1 clove garlic, crushed
1 med. onion, chopped
2 tsp. finely minced fresh
thyme
¼ tsp. black pepper
6 whole trout, ¾ lb. each, pan
dressed

6 bay leaves
4 T. melted butter
Juice of 2 lemons
Paprika

Mix garlic, onion, thyme and pepper. Blend together and spread on top each trout with spatula. Insert 1 whole bay leaf into each fish, then arrange in a single layer into a large well-oiled baking dish. Pour melted butter over fish and bake in preheated 400° oven for 12 to 15 minutes. Remove bay leaves and sprinkle with lemon juice and paprika before serving.

POULTRY & MEAT

Oven-Fried Chicken

3 tsp. salt
¼ tsp. pepper
1½ c. flour
½ c. paprika
1½ tsp. oregano

6 chicken breasts, skinned OR
1 chicken, cut up & skinned
1 to 2 c. buttermilk (you may
use sweet milk)
¾ c. melted butter

Mix salt, pepper, flour, paprika and oregano together. Dip a piece of chicken in buttermilk, then dip in seasoning mixture. Place pieces in foil-lined pan. Pour melted butter over the chicken. Bake at 350°, uncovered, until crisp brown (45 minutes to 1 hour).

CHICKEN & DUMPLINGS

2 env. Lipton's cream of
chicken Cup O' Soup
1 can Swanson's Chunk
Chicken Meat

½ pkg. mixed freeze-dried
vegetables
Water
1 c. Bisquick in a zip lock bag

Mix the soup, chicken and vegetables in a relatively deep pot with 2 to 3 cups water. Place on stove. Heat to simmering, stirring occasionally. While soup is heating, add water (see Bisquick box instructions for amount) to Bisquick and knead in the zip lock bag. When soup is hot, tear off a corner of the bag and squeeze out dumpling-size drops of Bisquick into the pot. Cover and cook for about 10 minutes on low heat.

EASY ROAST CHICKEN

1 T. flour
1 med. onion, cut into eighths
2 med. potatoes, cubed
4 med. carrots, sliced

2 stalks celery, sliced
4 to 5-lb. chicken
Seasoned salt
Pepper

Preheat oven to 350°. Shake flour into an oven bag (large size). Place in a 9 x 13-inch baking pan. Place vegetables in bag; turn bag to mix. Push vegetables to outer edge of bag. Sprinkle chicken with seasoned salt and pepper. Place chicken in center of vegetables, breast side up. Close bag with nylon tie; cut 6 slits in top of bag. Bake until chicken is tender, 1¼ to 1½ hours.

One-dish Chicken & Rice Bake

1 (10¾-oz.) can cream of
  mushroom soup
¼ tsp. paprika
¼ tsp. pepper

1 c. water
¾ c. uncooked regular long-
  grain rice
4 skinless, boneless chicken
  breasts

In 2-quart shallow baking dish mix soup, paprika, pepper, water and rice. Place chicken on rice mixture. Sprinkle with additional paprika and pepper. Cover. Bake at 375° for 45 minutes or until done. Serves 4.

Wild Rice Turkey Dish

1 (6-oz.) pkg. long-grain &
  wild rice mix
1 (10-oz.) can condensed
  cream of chicken soup
3 c. cubed, cooked turkey
  (leftover is good)
1 c. chopped celery
¼ c. chopped onion

1 (5-oz.) can water chestnuts,
  drained & sliced
1 (3-oz.) can chopped
  mushrooms, drained
3 T. soy sauce
1 c. water
1½ c. buttered soft bread
  crumbs

Cook rice mixture according to package directions. Blend in soup. Add turkey, celery, onion, water chestnuts, mushrooms, soy sauce and water. Mix well. Turn into 3-quart casserole. Sprinkle buttered bread crumbs on top. Bake at 350° for 1 hour. Makes 8 servings.

BEEF BRISKET

2-lb. brisket
1 env. onion soup mix

½ c. water
1 cooking bag

Use approximately ¼ pound meat per person to be served. Place brisket in cooking bag; sprinkle soup mix on top of meat. Put water in bag, toss. Fasten bag; cut slits in top. Bake at 275° to 300° for at least 4 hours. Roast is more tender if it is cooked longer at 225°. Reserve juice and skim off fat. Cool meat in refrigerator overnight. Slice while cold. Put in pan with juice reserved from cooking. Cover with foil and heat through, 30 to 45 minutes. (Don't set oven over 350°.)

POT ROAST WITH SOUR CREAM GRAVY

2 to 2½-lb. chuck roast
2 T. vegetable oil
½ c. water
3 med. potatoes, quartered
3 med. carrots, cut into 2-in.
  pieces

3 med. onions, quartered
1 T. all-purpose flour
1 (8-oz.) carton sour cream
¼ tsp. salt
⅛ tsp. pepper

Brown roast on both sides in oil in Dutch oven. Add water; cover. Reduce heat and simmer 2½ hours. Add potatoes, carrots and onions; simmer 30 minutes or until tender. Add more water, if needed. Remove roast and vegetables into 2-quart serving dish. Drain off drippings, leaving 2 tablespoons in pan. Reserve remaining drippings. Stir flour into drippings in pan; cook over medium heat until browned, stirring constantly. Add enough water to reserved drippings to make 1 cup. Stir into flour and cook until smooth and slightly thickened. Add sour cream, salt and pepper. Cook, stirring constantly, until thoroughly heated. Serve over roast.

HERBED PORK ROAST

1 c. soy sauce
2 T. lemon juice
2 garlic cloves, minced
2 tsp. dried tarragon
2 tsp. dried basil

1 tsp. dried chives
1 tsp. ground sage
1 tsp. pepper
1 (3½ to 4-lb.) boneless pork
  loin roast

In a large oven cooking bag, combine all ingredients except meat. Add roast; seal and turn to coat. Place bag in shallow roasting pan. Refrigerate overnight, turning bag several times. If using the cooking bag, make several ½-inch slits in top of bag. If not, remove roast from plastic bag and place in roasting pan. Pour marinade over roast. Cover the pan (leave uncovered if using cooking bag) and bake at 325° for 2½ to 3 hours or until a thermometer reads 160°. Let stand for 15 minutes before slicing. Yields 6 to 8 servings.

APPLE PORK CHOPS

1⅓ c. water
2 T. diced onions
¼ tsp. salt
2 T. butter
½ c. milk
1⅓ c. potato flakes
2 oz. shredded cheddar cheese

4 pork chops
2 T. butter
2 T. flour
2 T. brown sugar
1½ c. apple juice
1 apple, cored & ringed
Cinnamon

Preheat oven to 350°. Heat water, onions, salt and 2 tablespoons butter to full boil. Remove from heat. Add milk and potato flakes. Stir to desired consistency. Stir in cheese; set aside. In skillet, brown pork chops in 2 tablespoons butter. Salt to taste. Remove pork to baking dish. Stir flour and brown sugar into skillet to make a thick paste. Gradually add apple juice; cook and stir until thick. Place apple rings on top of each pork chop; sprinkle with cinnamon. Spoon potato mixture on top. Add skillet mixture over top. Bake 50 minutes.

DIJON MUSTARD LAMB

2 lg. cloves garlic
½ tsp. salt
2 T. Dijon-style prepared
  mustard
1 T. soy sauce
1½ tsp. ground rosemary,
  thyme or oregano

2 T. freshly squeezed lemon
  juice
¼ c. olive or peanut oil
2 racks lamb (1½ lbs. fully
  trimmed)

Mash garlic to a paste with the salt. Whisk in the mustard, soy sauce, herbs, lemon juice and then the oil to a mayonnaise-like cream. Trim most of the fat off of the lamb and score the fat side lightly. Paint mustard coating over top and sides. Fold a double strip of foil over the rib ends so they don't burn. Preheat oven to 500°. Set oven rack in upper middle level. Roast lamb for 10 minutes to sear. Reduce temperature to 400° and roast another 30 to 35 minutes or until cooked to your preference, basting periodically. Let set 5 minutes before carving.

CLASSIC LEG OF LAMB

6 to 9-lb. leg of lamb (bone in)
2 cloves garlic, cut into slivers
½ c. lemon juice

Salt & pepper to taste
1 tsp. dry rosemary, crumbled
½ tsp. dry basil leaves,
  crumbled

Place lamb in a shallow roasting pan. With a sharp knife, make slits in surface of lamb. Insert garlic slivers. Gently squeeze lemon juice over lamb, rubbing into slits and surface. Sprinkle with salt, pepper, rosemary and basil and rub seasonings into the surface. Roast in 325° oven for 25 minutes per pound or until meat thermometer registers 150° for medium rare. Remove from oven; cover and let stand 15 minutes before serving.

Sausage Gravy

1 lb. sage-flavored bulk pork
  sausage
2 T. onion, finely chopped
6 T. all-purpose flour
1 qt. milk

½ tsp. poultry seasoning
½ tsp. nutmeg
¼ tsp. salt
Dash of Worcestershire sauce
Dash of hot pepper sauce

Cook sausage in a large saucepan over medium to low heat. Add onion; cook and stir until onion is transparent. Drain, discarding all but 2 tablespoons of drippings. Stir in flour; cook over medium heat about 6 minutes or until mixture bubbles and turns golden. Stir in milk. Add remaining seasonings. Cook and stir until thickened. Serve on biscuits.

WILD GAME

DUCK & WILD RICE CASSEROLE

2 med. ducks
Water
3 stalks celery
1 onion, halved
Salt
Pepper
6-oz. pkg. seasoned wild &
  long grain rice
½ c. chopped onion

½ c. margarine
¼ c. flour
4 oz. mushrooms, sliced
1½ c. half & half
1 T. parsley, chopped
1½ tsp. salt
¼ tsp. pepper
Slivered almonds

Boil ducks in water, celery, onion halves, salt and pepper for 1 hour or until tender. Reserve broth. Cube meat. Cook the rice according to instructions on package. Saute onions in margarine; stir in flour. Drain mushrooms; reserve mushroom juice and add enough broth to make 1½ cups liquid. Add mushrooms to onions; add 1½ cups liquid to onions. Add duck cubes, rice, half & half, parsley, salt and pepper to the onions. Place in a greased 2-quart casserole dish. Sprinkle almonds on top. Cover and bake at 350° for 15 to 20 minutes. Uncover and bake 5 to 10 minutes more or until very hot. Serves 6.

CREAMED DOVE CASSEROLE

12 dove breasts
Flour
Salt & pepper

Vegetable oil
2 cans cream of mushroom
soup

Roll dove breasts in flour, salt and pepper. Brown in vegetable oil. Remove and place in soup. Simmer for 45 minutes on low heat (or until doves are tender). Remove from soup and remove meat from bones. Cut meat into small pieces and mix back into soup mixture. Serve over rice or biscuits!

SOUTHWEST DUCK WITH SCALLOPS

4 duck breasts, cooked &
 diced
1 T. oil
4 T. barbecue sauce
8 scallops
8 slices bacon
4 oz. onions, chopped

10 oz. corn
Salt & pepper
¼ c. cream
1 T. red pepper puree

Saute duck in oil and brown; then add barbecue sauce. In separate pan, wrap scallops in bacon and saute until cooked. Add to duck. Mix onions, corn, salt, pepper and cream. Cook in a separate pan until tender. Puree in blender. Put corn mixture on plate; top with duck. Garnish with red pepper puree and serve with rice.

Baked Pheasant

Flour
Salt & pepper to taste
Pheasants, cut up
Oil
Cream of chicken soup

Evaporated milk
Water
Milk
Minced onion (opt.)

Mix flour, salt and pepper together. Dip pheasant in flour mixture; fry in oil. Save browning. **Gravy:** Add 1 can soup plus ½ can evaporated milk and 1 can of water to browning. Have enough gravy to cover all pieces of pheasant. Put into roaster and bake 1 to 1½ hours in 350° oven until meat is tender. Keep meat, covered, with gravy mixture. Add more water or regular milk to thin, if necessary as gravy thickens as it bakes.

Roast Goose With Mushroom Gravy

1 (5 to 8-lb.) goose
Garlic salt
Paprika
1½ stalks celery, chopped
1 carrot, chopped
1 med. onion, chopped
Butter

4 T. flour
½ tsp. rosemary
¼ tsp. thyme
1¼ tsp. salt
1 c. sour cream
1 can mushrooms, drained

Season goose inside and out with garlic salt and paprika. Place on rack in shallow pan and bake, uncovered, for 1 hour at 325°. Boil giblets in water until tender. Cook celery, carrots and onion in small amount of butter until soft. Stir in 2 tablespoons flour and 1 cup stock from giblets. Add rosemary, thyme and salt. Stir remaining flour into sour cream and blend into gravy. Add mushrooms. Remove goose. Place in a roasting pan and pour gravy mixture over goose. Cover and bake an additional 2 hours or until tender.

STIR-FRIED VENISON

1 c. diced bacon
3 to 4 cloves fresh garlic
2 c. diced broccoli
1 c. sliced onion

1 c. chopped celery
2 to 3-lbs. cubed venison
2 T. soy sauce
Salt & pepper to taste

Fry bacon until brown; remove and set aside. Into bacon grease, add garlic, broccoli, onion and celery. Cook until slightly tender. Remove from grease and set aside. Add venison and fry until done. Add bacon and cooked vegetables. Stir and add soy sauce. Remove from heat. Serve with wild rice.

VENISON BURGER

3 lbs. ground venison
1 env. onion soup mix

¼ c. milk
2 T. flour

Mix and make into patties. Fry or broil.

COUNTRY-FRIED VENISON STEAKS

2 lbs. venison round or sirloin
  tip steaks (½ to 1 in. thick)
½ c. flour
3 T. shortening

Salt & pepper
2 cans condensed cream of
  mushroom soup
Water

Trim all fat from the steaks; cut into pieces approximately 3-inch squares. Using a meat mallet, pound flour into both sides of the steaks. Melt shortening in a large skillet and brown meat slowly and thoroughly over medium heat (15 to 20 minutes). Season to taste with salt and pepper. As pieces are browned, transfer them to a 2 to 3-quart deep casserole dish. Blend the mushroom soup in a blender until creamy. Pour this mixture over the steak. Add enough water to cover all pieces of steak. Cover and bake until tender (approximately 2½ hours) in 350° oven, adding water as necessary.

JALAPEÑO VENISON BACKSTRAP

2 to 3 lbs. venison backstrap
Jar sliced jalapeño peppers
Sm. bottle Italian dressing
7 to 8 strips bacon

Potatoes, carrots, onions, bell
  peppers
Salt & pepper to taste

Wash and clean backstrap, removing all white muscle. Cut backstrap in half (lengthwise). Place jalapeños between cuts of meat. Pour ½ bottle Italian dressing over meat. Wrap cuts of meat with bacon. Hold together with toothpicks. Place in foil-lined 13 x 9-inch baking dish. Cut up potatoes, carrots, onions and bell peppers. Salt and pepper to taste. Pour remaining dressing over vegetables. Cover with foil and seal. Bake at 350° for 1 to 1½ hours.

SIDE DISHES & SALADS

Oven Fries

1½ lbs. baking potatoes,   1 T. vegetable oil
  peeled & cut into thin strips   ½ tsp. salt

Preheat oven to 450°. Combine all ingredients in a bowl; toss well. Arrange the potatoes in a single layer on a baking sheet. Bake at 450° for 35 minutes or until golden.

Chili Fries

2 tsp. chili powder   ¼ tsp. garlic powder
½ dried oregano   ¼ tsp. ground cumin

Mix these ingredients into oven fries mixture and follow same baking directions as oven fries.

Cheese Fries

¼ tsp. salt   ¼ tsp. paprika
1 T. grated Parmesan cheese   ¼ tsp. pepper
¼ tsp. garlic powder

Mix these ingredients into oven fries mixture (minus salt) and follow same baking directions as oven fries.

Hash Brown Casserole

1 pkg. frozen hash brown
  potatoes
1 stick margarine
1 can cream of mushroom
  soup
1 can cream of chicken soup

½ soup can milk
¼ tsp. salt
¼ tsp. pepper
1 c. shredded cheddar cheese

Combine partially thawed hash browns and melted margarine. Combine soups, milk, salt and pepper. Pour over hash brown potatoes. Stir in cheese. Bake in a greased 9 x 13-inch baking dish for 1 hour at 350°.

Make-ahead Mashed Potatoes

5 lbs. peeled and boiled
  potatoes
¼ lb. butter or margarine
3 oz. half & half
8 oz. sour cream

4 T. milk
1 beaten egg
Salt & pepper to taste
Parsley, chopped
Salt and pepper, to taste

Mash potatoes thoroughly with electric mixer. Mix in butter, half & half, sour cream, milk, egg, salt and pepper. Sprinkle chopped parsley on top. Refrigerate overnight. Before baking, bring to room temperature. Bake for 1 hour at 350°. Serves 12 to 16.

"The 24th of July was a day long to be remembered ... as the anniversary of the arrival of the pioneers two years previous. To behold twelve or fifteen hundred feet of tables, filling the bower and all adjoining grounds, loaded with all luxuries of the field and gardens, and nearly all the varieties that any vegetable market in the world could produce ..."
    ~ Local newspaper

RUSTIC HOME-FRIED POTATOES

2 T. margarine
3 med. potatoes, thinly sliced
1 med. sweet onion, halved &
  thinly sliced
2 cloves garlic, minced

2 T. parsley, dried
1 T. rosemary, dried &
  crushed
¼ tsp. salt
⅛ tsp. ground red pepper
⅛ tsp. ground black pepper

In a large skillet melt margarine. Layer the sliced potatoes, onion and garlic in the skillet. Sprinkle with parsley, rosemary, salt, ground red pepper and ground black pepper. Cook potato mixture, covered, over medium heat for 8 minutes. Continue cooking, uncovered, for 8 to 10 minutes more or until potatoes are tender and brown, turning frequently.

ROASTED NEW POTATOES

24 sm. new potatoes
Cooking spray
¼ c. Italian-seasoned bread
  crumbs

¼ c. Parmesan cheese
¾ tsp. paprika

Cook unpeeled potatoes in boiling water 15 minutes. Drain and cool. Quarter potatoes and coat cut sides with cooking spray. Combine bread crumbs, cheese and paprika. Dredge cut sides of potatoes with bread crumb mixture. Arrange in a single layer on a baking sheet coated with cooking spray. Bake at 450° for 15 minutes.

BAKED BEANS

2 to 3 cans baked beans
¾ c. dark brown sugar
2 to 3 T. catsup
2 to 3 T. barbecue sauce
2 T. vinegar

1 T. prepared mustard
1 lg. onion
1 med. green pepper, sliced
1 c. colby cheese, cubed
4 to 5 slices bacon

Combine beans, sugar, catsup, barbecue sauce, vinegar and mustard until well blended. Add onion, green pepper and cheese; stir evenly throughout beans. Place bacon slices on top. Bake at 400° for 1 hour or until onion and green pepper are soft and bacon is golden brown.

BISCUITS & BEANS

1 lb. ground beef
1 tsp. salt
1 can pork & beans
¾ c. barbecue sauce
2 T. brown sugar

1 T. instant minced onion
1 can refrigerated biscuits
1 c. (4 oz.) shredded cheddar
  or mozzarella cheese

Brown beef in skillet; drain. Stir in salt, beans, barbecue sauce, sugar and onion. Heat until bubbly. Spoon into a 2-quart casserole. Place biscuits on top of meat mixture. Bake at 375° for 25 to 30 minutes. Five minutes before it's done, sprinkle cheese on top. Yield: 4 to 6 servings.

Corn Casserole

16-oz. can whole corn
16-oz. can cream corn
8-oz. carton sour cream
2 eggs, beaten

⅓ c. sugar
½ c. oil
1 box Jiffy cornbread mix

Mix all ingredients together. Pour into 9 x 13-inch pan. Bake at 350° for 1 hour.

Corn Fritters

1 c. sifted all-purpose flour
1½ tsp. baking powder
2 T. sugar
1½ tsp. salt

1 egg, beaten
⅓ c. milk
1 T. shortening
2 c. corn niblets, drained

Mix flour, baking powder, sugar and salt. Add egg, milk and shortening. Beat until smooth. Fold in corn niblets. Drop by teaspoonfuls in hot grease. Fry until brown.

STUFFED ACORN SQUASH

2 acorn squash
½ c. chopped onion
1 clove garlic, crushed
1 stalk celery, chopped
¼ c. chopped walnuts
¼ c. sunflower seeds
½ tsp. rubbed sage

3 T. butter
½ tsp. thyme
1 c. crumbled wheat bread
Juice from ½ lemon
½ c. raisins
½ c. shredded cheddar cheese

Split two squash lengthwise. Remove the seeds and place face down on an oiled baking sheet. Bake in a 350° oven for 30 minutes or until tender. Prepare filling while squash is baking. **Filling:** Saute onion, garlic, celery, nuts and seeds in butter. Cook over low heat until onions are clear. Add remaining ingredients except cheese. Cook, stirring over low heat 5 to 8 minutes. Remove from heat and stir in cheese. Pack stuffing into squash hollows. Cover and bake in 350° oven for 25 minutes.

CORN SOUFFLE

3 T. butter
4 T. flour
1 c. milk
¾ tsp. salt

Dash of pepper
½ tsp. dry mustard
2½ c. corn
½ c. American cheese
4 eggs, separated

Blend butter and flour together. Add milk, salt, pepper and mustard. Cook until thickened, stirring constantly. Add corn and remove from heat. Stir in the cheese and well-beaten egg yolks. Fold in stiffly beaten egg whites. Pour into a medium-sized casserole. Set in a shallow pan of hot water and bake at 350° for 1 hour or until firm and well browned. Serves 8.

PECAN CRUMBLE SWEET POTATOES

½ c. unsifted all-purpose flour
½ c. firmly packed light
  brown sugar
½ tsp. ground allspice

¼ c. butter or margarine
2½ to 3 lbs. sweet potatoes
⅓ c. pecan halves
½ c. maple syrup

Preheat oven to 350°. In medium bowl combine flour, sugar and allspice; mix well. With pastry blender or 2 knives, cut in butter until mixture forms coarse crumbs; set aside. Grease 2-quart shallow baking or casserole dish. Cut potatoes in ¼-inch thick diagonal slices. Place about ⅓ of potato slices in baking dish; sprinkle with ½ cup of crumb mixture. Layer remaining potato slices, slightly overlapping, on top. Sprinkle with remaining crumb mixture and the pecans. Drizzle with maple syrup. Bake, lightly covered with foil, 45 minutes; remove foil. Cook until potatoes are tender, about 10 minutes. Makes 6 servings.

LAYERED SALAD

2 med. heads lettuce, torn
6 hard-boiled eggs, sliced
1 lb. bacon, cooked &
  crumbled
1 (8-oz.) can water chestnuts,
  sliced
1 (10-oz.) pkg. frozen peas,
  thawed

½ pkg. Hidden Valley Ranch
  dressing mix
1 c. mayonnaise
½ c. sour cream

In large salad bowl, layer lettuce, eggs, bacon, water chestnuts and peas in order given. Combine Ranch dressing mix, mayonnaise and sour cream. Spread over top of vegetables, sealing to edge of bowl. Cover tightly and refrigerate overnight.

COLESLAW WITH APPLES

3 c. thinly sliced green
  cabbage
2 c. thinly sliced red cabbage
3 green onions, green & white
  portion thinly sliced
1 carrot, shredded

1 red pepper, diced
1 green pepper, diced
1 apple, peeled, cored & thinly
  sliced

Dressing:

½ c. mayonnaise
¼ c. thinly sliced green onion
2 T. maple syrup
1 T. Dijon mustard
2 tsp. fresh lemon juice

½ c. sour cream
2 T. red wine vinegar
1 T. vegetable oil
1 T. poppy seed
Salt & pepper to taste

Combine the cabbages, green onions, carrot, peppers and apple in a large bowl; toss. Combine all the dressing ingredients in a separate bowl; mix well. Pour the dressing over the cabbage mixture; toss well to blend. Cover and refrigerate for 1 hour before serving. Serves 8.

HONEY BEE AMBROSIA

4 med. oranges, peeled &
  sliced crosswise
3 bananas, sliced
½ c. orange juice

¼ c. honey
2 T. lemon juice
¼ c. flaked coconut
Maraschino cherry halves
  (opt.)

Combine oranges and bananas in a medium bowl, tossing lightly. Combine orange juice, honey and lemon juice; pour over fruit and mix well. Sprinkle with coconut; cover and chill at least 1 hour. Garnish with maraschino cherries, if desired. Yield: 6 servings.

DESSERTS

CANDIED APPLES

6 popsicle sticks
6 med. apples
1 c. sugar
¾ c. dark brown sugar

1 c. light cream
2 T. butter
1 tsp. vanilla extract
Chopped nuts, optional

Place a stick in the end of each apple. Combine sugars, cream and butter in heavy saucepan. Cook, without stirring, over low heat until very hard ball stage or until candy thermometer reaches between 254° and 260°. Remove from heat and stir in vanilla. Dip apples into syrup as fast as possible. If desired, you may roll them in chopped nuts. Place upright on well-greased cookie sheet to cool.

HARD TACK

4 eggs
2 c. sugar
2 c. dates, stoned
1½ c. nutmeats

1 T. water
Flour
Powdered sugar

Cream eggs and sugar together. Then add dates, nuts and water. Add enough flour to make a stiff batter. Spread thinly on waxed paper in long biscuit pan. Bake until it is a light brown all over. Turn out and cut in squares and dip in powdered sugar while hot.

Campfire Peaches

Peaches   **Allspice**
Nutmeg   **Lemon juice**
Cinnamon   **Molasses**

Cut hole in peach from stem and carefully remove pit, without cutting all the way through the peach. Sprinkle cavity heavily with nutmeg, cinnamon and allspice; spread evenly with finger. Sprinkle lemon juice into cavity. Fill cavity halfway with molasses. Wrap peach in aluminum foil and heat by the fire until it feels soft and mushy. Peel foil away and eat with spoon, or serve over ice cream. **Note:** This works well with apples, pears, apricots and many other fruits.

INDIAN PUDDING

2 qt. milk
2 c. sugar
1⅓ c. coarse cornmeal or grits
1 tsp. salt
1½ tsp. cinnamon

1 tsp. nutmeg
½ c. butter
4 or 5 eggs
1 c. (or more) raisins

Put one quart of milk in saucepan to heat. Mix sugar, cornmeal, salt, cinnamon and nutmeg well; add to milk. Stir until it boils. Add butter and rest of milk and the eggs, which have been beaten separately. Divide into 2 large or 3 small pudding pans. Bake at 325° for 2 hours. When pudding begins to set, stir in raisins. If pudding seems too stiff, add more milk as it bakes or when reheating. Can be kept in refrigerator a long time.

Indian Pudding Sauce:

2 T. butter
2 tsp. cinnamon
¼ tsp. nutmeg
¼ tsp. ginger

2 c. sugar
2 T. cornstarch
2 c. water

Melt margarine. Add cinnamon, nutmeg and ginger; boil a minute. Mix sugar and cornstarch, then add to margarine mix. Add water and boil until thick.

RICE PUDDING WITH RAISINS

4 c. 1% milk
½ c. uncooked long-grain
  white rice
½ c. raisins
1 lg. egg

2 lg. egg whites
¾ c. sugar
⅓ c. evaporated skim milk
1½ tsp. vanilla extract
Ground cinnamon

Put milk, rice and raisins in a large, heavy saucepan or Dutch oven and bring to a boil over medium-high heat. Reduce heat to low and simmer 20 minutes, stirring often, until rice is almost tender. Meanwhile, whisk egg, egg whites, sugar and evaporated milk in a medium-sized bowl until blended. Stirring constantly, gradually add to hot rice mixture. Stir over low heat about 3 minutes, until slightly thickened. Remove from heat; stir in vanilla. Pour pudding into shallow dish or individual dessert glasses. Serve warm or cover and chill until ready to serve. Just before serving, sprinkle with cinnamon.

GINGERBREAD

1 c. flour
½ c. brown sugar
2 tsp. ground ginger
1 tsp. ground cinnamon
¼ tsp. ground cloves
¼ tsp. freshly ground pepper
½ tsp. salt

1 tsp. baking soda
1 T. unsweetened cocoa
½ c. molasses
¼ c. plain yogurt
¼ c. vegetable oil
1 egg, lightly beaten

Preheat oven to 350°. Coat with nonstick cooking spray, the bottom of an 8-inch round baking pan. Line bottom of pan with waxed paper cut to fit and coat paper with nonstick cooking spray. In a food processor, combine flour, sugar, ginger, cinnamon, cloves, pepper, salt, baking soda and cocoa. Pulse on and off 2 or 3 times to blend. Add molasses, yogurt, oil and egg; pulse on and off 4 to 5 times or until flour disappears. Pour batter into prepared pan and smooth top with rubber spatula. Bake for 25 to 30 minutes until wooden pick inserted in the center comes out clean. Cool on wire rack before removing from pan. Makes 8 servings.

STRAWBERRY SHORTCAKE

2½ c. plain sifted flour
3 tsp. baking powder
1 tsp. salt
½ c. shortening
1½ c. sugar

1 c. milk
2 eggs
1 tsp. vanilla
2 pkgs. frozen strawberries,
   sweetened

Sift and measure flour twice. Add baking powder and salt; sift again. Add shortening, sugar and ¾ cup milk. Beat for about 2 minutes with mixer. Add eggs, vanilla and ¼ cup milk. Beat for 1 minute. Grease oblong cake pan. Pour mixture into pan. Bake at 375° for approximately 30 minutes; let cool. Poke holes all over cake with toothpick. Blend strawberries. Pour berries over cake. Refrigerate until serving.

GOOSEBERRY COBBLER

2 c. gooseberries   1 T. butter
1½ c. sugar   1 T. lemon juice
¾ c. water   Lattice pastry strips
2 T. minute tapioca

Mix gooseberries, sugar, water and tapioca. Add butter and lemon juice. Pour into baking dish. Top with pastry strips. Bake at 350° for 45 minutes.

BLACKBERRY COBBLER

Berry Mixture:

5 c. fresh blackberries   1 tsp. grated lemon rind
¾ c. sugar   1 T. lemon juice
2 T. flour   1 tsp. vanilla

Topping:

1 c. flour   2 T. lemon juice
1 tsp. baking powder   2 T. margarine, melted
½ tsp. soda   1 tsp. vanilla
½ c. plain nonfat yogurt   2 egg whites

Combine all berry mixture ingredients and stir gently. Spoon into an 11 x 7 x 2-inch baking dish coated with cooking spray. In separate bowl combine flour, baking powder and soda. Stir in yogurt, lemon juice, margarine, vanilla and egg whites just until dry ingredients are moistened. Drop by tablespoons onto berry mixture. Bake at 400° for 30 minutes. Serve warm. Makes 8 servings.

Apple Dumplings Deluxe

1 beaten egg
8 oz. carton sour cream
2 c. flour
2 T. sugar
2 tsp. baking powder
¼ tsp. baking soda
¼ tsp. salt
4 c. peeled & thinly sliced
  apples
¼ c. sugar

½ tsp. cinnamon
¼ tsp. nutmeg
1½ c. water
1¼ c. brown sugar
1 c. sugar
2 T. cornstarch
2 T. lemon juice
2 T. butter

Dough: Combine egg and sour cream. In small bowl, mix flour, 2 tablespoons sugar, baking powder, baking soda and salt. Add to sour cream; mix well. On a floured surface, roll dough into a 12-inch square. Spread apples on top. In a small bowl, combine ¼ cup sugar, cinnamon and nutmeg. Sprinkle on top of the apples. Carefully roll up dough. Cut into 12 (1-inch) slices. Place cut side down in greased baking dish. Stir together: water, brown sugar, 1 cup sugar, cornstarch and lemon juice. Pour over slices in pan. Dot with butter. Bake, uncovered, in a 350° oven for 35 to 40 minutes or until golden brown.

Chocolate Fried Pies

1 recipe biscuit dough
3 T. cocoa
2 T. butter, melted

1½ c. sugar
2 T. canola oil

Make your favorite (2 cups of flour) biscuit recipe. Let the dough rest at room temperature at least 2 hours. Divide dough into 8 parts; form into balls; flatten and roll out into circles, about ⅛ inch thick. Mix the cocoa, melted butter and sugar together; divide evenly over the circles. Fold the dough over to make half circles. Pinch the edges together. Press pattern along the edges with a fork. Preheat oil in a large skillet over medium heat; brown each pie on both sides. Add more oil as needed. Serve warm or cold.

CHEESY APPLE PIE

Cheese Pastry:

2 c. flour
½ to 1 c. grated sharp cheese
½ tsp. salt

⅔ c. cold butter
4 to 5 T. ice water

In food processor or by hand, mix flour, cheese and salt. Cut in butter. Add ice water slowly with processor running, or mix lightly with fork. Wrap and chill. Flour board very well. Roll half of dough for bottom crust. Carefully transfer to 9-inch pie pan. Roll remaining half of dough for top crust; set aside.

Filling:

6 or 7 tart apples
¾ c. sugar
2 T. flour
1 tsp. ground cinnamon

⅛ tsp. ground nutmeg
⅛ tsp. salt
4 T. butter

Pare and slice apples to ¼-inch thickness (approximately 6 cups). Combine sugar, flour, cinnamon, nutmeg and salt; mix with apples. Spoon apple mixture into bottom of pastry crust. Dot with butter. Place reserved pastry top over apples. Pinch edges together and flute. Bake at 400° for 1 hour or until apples are done. If fluted edges begin to brown too much, cover with foil. Serve plain or with vanilla ice cream.

HOMEMADE ROCKY ROAD ICE CREAM

2 c. milk
1¾ c. sugar
2 c. half & half
4 c. whipping cream
1½ c. chocolate chips
6 squares semi-sweet
  chocolate, melted

½ tsp. salt
1 T. vanilla
2 c. miniature marshmallows
1 c. pecans

Mix all ingredients. Put in freezer container and freeze until firm.

BEEHIVES

½ c. honey
1 egg, beaten
1 tsp. vanilla
2 c. coconut

1 c. walnuts
1 c. dates, chopped
2 c. flour

Mix together honey, egg, vanilla, coconut and walnuts. In separate
bowl mix dates and flour. Put all together and mix well. Drop on
greased baking sheet and bake 12 minutes at 325°.

MICROWAVE CARAMEL CORN

1 c. brown sugar
½ c. margarine
¼ c. light corn syrup
¼ tsp. salt

½ tsp. baking soda
½ tsp. vanilla
3 to 4 qt. popped corn

Combine sugar, margarine, syrup and salt in 2-quart glass dish. Microwave on high for 2 minutes; stir. Continue to microwave, uncovered, to boiling. Boil 3 minutes. Remove from microwave. Add soda and vanilla; stir well. Put popped corn in large brown grocery bag. Add syrup mixture and close bag loosely. Microwave on high for 1½ minutes; shake. Microwave another 1½ minutes; shake. Microwave 45 seconds; shake. Microwave 30 seconds; shake. Spread on waxed paper to cool.

PRESERVING

CROCKPOT APPLE BUTTER

7 c. applesauce
2 c. apple cider
1½ c. honey

1 tsp. cinnamon
½ tsp. ground cloves
1 tsp. ground allspice

Requires a large crockpot. May halve recipe for a small crockpot. In a large bowl, whisk all ingredients together. Pour into a crockpot. Cook on low setting for 14 hours. Makes 4 pints. Freezes well in plastic containers. Keep refrigerated.

HUCKLEBERRY JAM

3 qt. huckleberries
1 c. water
½ c. fresh lemon juice

1 pkg. pectin
6 c. sugar

Grind huckleberries or crush thoroughly until reduced to a pulp. Add water, if necessary, to make 4¾ cups fruit and juice. Measure prepared fruit and lemon juice into 6 to 8-quart saucepan. Add pectin to fruit, mixing thoroughly. Place fruit mixture over high heat and bring to a full rolling boil, stirring constantly. Stir in sugar, mixing well. Bring to a full rolling boil, stirring constantly. Boil 4 minutes. Remove from heat and skim off any foam. Fill jars to ⅛ inch of tops. Cover quickly with flat lids and screw bands on tightly. Invert jars for 5 minutes, then turn jars upright. After 1 hour check seals.

PEACH CONSERVE

4 lbs. fresh peaches, peeled,
   pitted & diced
48 dried apricot halves, cut in
   sm. pieces
3 c. light brown sugar
3 c. granulated sugar

1 tsp. cinnamon
1 c. blanched almonds,
   toasted & chopped
½ c. water
1 tsp. almond extract

Combine peaches, apricots, sugars and cinnamon. Cook over high heat for 15 minutes until thickened, stirring occasionally. Remove from heat and stir in almonds, water and almond extract. Pour into hot, sterilized half-pint jars and seal. Makes 8 (half-pints). This makes a wonderful sauce over pound cake, biscuits or ice cream.

Homemade Sauerkraut

1 T. salt
Shredded cabbage

1 T. sugar
Boiling water

For quarts: Put salt in the bottom of a quart jar. Pack the jar with shredded cabbage. Press down cabbage each time it is added to the jar. Add sugar. Fill with boiling water. Put on lid and set aside to ferment. It will take several days for the fermentation to stop. When fermentation stops, put jar in boiling water bath for 10 minutes to seal. Clean the top of the jar so lids will seal tightly.

Corn For The Freezer

10 c. raw corn, cut from cob
1/3 c. butter
2 tsp. salt

1/2 c. sugar
2 c. water

Mix all ingredients. Put in 9 x 13-inch baking pan in 350° oven for 45 minutes. Cool in ice water or refrigerate until well chilled. Put in cartons and freeze.

Dried Tomatoes

Cut in slices and spread ripe tomatoes out on cookie sheets. Put them in the oven. Keep the temperature below 165° (the pilot light in a gas oven may be all you need) and leave them alone. It should take between 15 to 24 hours to dry, depending on your oven. Store them in bags or glass jars in a cold, dark place.

JERKY

Up to 10 lbs. meat
2 qt. water
½ pt. vinegar

2 c. salt
2 T. pepper
Steak sauce

Boil meat, water, vinegar, salt and pepper for 5 minutes. Roll flat with rolling pin. If color is red, boil longer; should be a grey-brown color. Cook in 200° oven with cracked door until almost dry, 1½ hours. Should not break when bent. After dried, paint both sides with steak sauce. Repaint if more flavor needed.

BEEF JERKY

Flank steak
Soy sauce

Garlic salt
Lemon pepper

Trim fat off steak. Slice with grain into strips, ¼ to ½ inch thick. Coat with soy sauce. On a cookie sheet with cake cooling rack, lay strips across rack in a single layer. Sprinkle with garlic salt and lemon pepper. Bake 8 to 10 hours at 150°-175°. Store in an air-tight container.

COLD-PACKED DEER

Cut deer meat in 2-inch pieces. Put in uncovered roaster in oven at 250°. Keep stirring meat until all pink is gone. Put 2 beef bouillon cubes in each jar. Pack meat tightly and add water or juice to 1 inch of the top. Process 50 minutes in a pressure canner.

Pioneer Home Remedies

"Sod House"

PIONEER HOME REMEDIES

"Inasmuch as any man drinketh wine or strong
drink among you, behold it is not good ... Strong
drinks are not for the belly, but for the washing of
your bodies. And again, tobacco is not for the body,
neither for the belly, and is not good for man, but is
an herb for bruises and all sick cattle, to be used
with judgement and skill. ... And all saints who
remember to keep and do these sayings, walking in
obedience to the commandments, shall receive health
in their navel and marrow to their bones; And shall
find wisdom and great treasures of knowledge, even
hidden treasures ..."

~ Doctrine and Covenants, Section 89

Early Mormon medicinal practices embraced two similar philosophies:
Thompsonian medicine and faith healing. Thompsonian medicine was
developed by Samuel Thompson, who promoted the use of herbs, hot
baths and dietary moderation. This type of medicine was practiced by
several who were closely associated with Joseph Smith.

Faith healing among Mormons originated with Brigham Young. Young
instructed the people when their children were sick that "instead of
calling for a doctor, you should administer to them by the laying on of
hands and anointing with oil, and give them mild food and herbs and
medicine that you understand."

While keeping both Thompsonian and faith healing practices in mind, the
pioneers dealt with medicine the best way a migratory group could; they
packed only the herbs and solutions that would travel well without
taking up too much room, and relied on the land to supply the rest.
Guided by their faith and intuition, they began the journey that taught
them more than they could have ever imagined.

Often, new cures had to be found for ailments the pioneers had not
encountered before they departed on the Trail. At times, the plants, herbs
and other ingredients comprising the supposed cure seemed even more
harmful than the ailment it was designed to remedy. Ingredients such as
garlic, coal, castor oil, turpentine and kerosene were quite common in cures.

Pioneer Home Remedies

Medicinal Remedies

Chest Cold Medicine

Use goose grease and turpentine for a chest cold.

Horehound Candy For Coughs

Boil two ounces of dried horehound in a pint and a half of water for about half an hour; strain and add three and a half pounds of brown sugar; boil over a hot fire until sufficiently hard; pour out in flat, well-greased tins and mark into sticks or small squares with a knife as soon as cool enough to retain its shape.

Cold & Headache Medicine

When you have a cold, grease your chest with this mixture: 1 teaspoon camphor, 1 teaspoon turpentine, 2 teaspoons kerosene, 2 teaspoons lard or warm grease. For a sick headache, take the juice of half a lemon in a cup of black coffee without sugar and cream. It is an excellent remedy.

HOMEMADE COUGH MEDICINE

4 T. sugar   3 T. water
3 T. honey   Juice of ½ lemon

Mix all ingredients and bring to a boil. Pour into medicine bottle. Take
¼ teaspoon every ½ hour.

COUGH REMEDIES

1. Use the syrup made by boiling water with one onion and add
horehound.

2. Mash onions with sugar and eat this for a bad cough.

COUGH SYRUP

1 oz. Boneset   1 qt. water
1 oz. Slippery Elm   1 pt. molasses
1 oz. stick licorice   ½ lb. rock candy
1 oz. flax seed

Simmer water, Boneset, Slippery Elm, licorice and flax seed until
strength is extracted; strain. Add molasses and rock candy. Simmer
together and bottle tight.

GRANNY RAG

Mix together hog lard, tablespoon turpentine and tablespoon coal oil.
Heat on stove until hot. Dip a heavy flannel or a piece of old union
suit. Place on chest and pin in place with safety pin. When cooled
down, reheat and reapply.

Sore Throat Remedy

4 T. molasses   **1 T. paregoric**
2 T. olive oil

Mix all together. Take 1 teaspoonful when needed.

Nosebleed

1. Take a small piece of lead and bore a hole in it. Put a string through the hole, tie it and wear it around your neck. Your nose won't bleed again.

2. Place a coin directly under the nose between the upper lip and the gum and press tightly.

3. Hang a pair of pot hooks about your neck.

Pneumonia

1. To bring down the fever, put some quinine and hog lard on a cloth and put it on your chest.

2. Give the person two teaspoonfuls of oil rendered from a skunk.

3. Make an onion poultice to make the fever break.

RHEUMATISM

1. Drink a tea made from the seeds or leaves of the alfalfa plant.

2. Cook garlic in your food to ease the pain.

3. Carry a buckeye or an Irish potato until it gets hard.

STOMACH TROUBLE

1. Make a tea of wild peppermint and drink it.

2. Drink some blackberry juice.

3. Drink some juice from kraut left over after cooking.

EARACHE

1. Dissolve table salt in lukewarm water and pour this into ear. This dissolves the wax which is causing the pain.

2. Put either wet ashes wrapped in a cloth or hot ashes in a sack. Put on ear and hold there.

3. Roast cabbage stalks and squeeze the juice into ear.

4. Warm a spoonful of urine and put a few drops in ear.

5. Hold your head close to a hot lamp.

6. Put a few ashes in an old rag. Dampen it with hot water and sleep with your head on it.

Eye Ailments

Put a few drops of castor oil in eye.

Eyewash

Gun powder dissolved in water for eyewash.

Fever

Boil two roots of wild ginger in a cup of water; strain and drink.

Measles

Any herb tea will break them out.

Puncture Wound

1. Pour kerosene oil over the cut or soak it in same three times a day. This will also remove the soreness.

2. Mix lard with soot from the chimney, thin with turpentine and pack around the wound.

3. Chop up red beet leaves and make a plaster to spread over wound.

Fretful Child

Boil catnip leaves to make a tea and give the child about a quarter cup. Use one cup of leaves to a pint of water to make him sleep.

Headaches

1. Tie a flour sack around your head.

2. Put turpentine and beef tallow in a bandage and tie it lightly around your head.

3. Smear brow with crushed onions.

4. When you get you hair cut, gather up all the clippings. Bury them. Old-timers would never allow their hair to be burned or thrown away as it was too valuable.

Heart Trouble

Eat ramps and garlic. You can eat them cooked or raw.

Recipe For Curing Hiccup

Hiccup can usually be stopped very quickly by taking a teaspoonful of granulated sugar and vinegar. If it does not give relief, repeat the dose.

Inflammation

Bind salty fat meat to a stone bruise or a thorn in the foot to draw out the inflammation. A poultice of clay will do the same thing. To kill infection, pour some turpentine or kerosene mixed with sugar on the affected area.

Infection

For drawing out infection on burns, use raw grated potatoes.

Boil Or Sore

For a festering boil or sore, put a hot onion over area and let soak.

Scrapes & Abrasions

Smear rabbit fat over raw areas.

Constipated Infants

Use a short piece of geranium stem as a suppository.

Bugs

For head lice (cooties), shingle hair close and use kerosene. For chinches or bed bugs, burn sulfur in a closed house.

Bee Stings

Put mud or red clay on area.

FOOD FOR INVALIDS

The following recipes were extensively used by the pioneers to provide nourishment for their loved ones during and after an illness.

Currant Water

Stir a tablespoonful of currant jelly into a glass of water. Sweeten slightly, if desired. When currant juice is obtainable, use three tablespoons of the juice and enough water to dilute to the desired acidity. Acid drinks are most refreshing for a fever.

Rice Water

Wash four tablespoons of rice. Add three cups of cold water. Place it on the fire and cook for half an hour. Season with salt; strain and serve.

Barley Water

Wash five tablespoons of pearl barley. Add four cups of cold water; place it on the fire and boil slowly for two hours. Strain, and when cold, season with a little salt, or, if not hurtful, a little lemon and sugar.

TOAST WATER

Toast two or three slices of stale bread until brown all through, but not at all scorched. Break the toast in small pieces and put a cupful of it into a pitcher, using only the toast which is thoroughly brown. Pour on the toast three cups of boiling water; let this stand for ten minutes; strain and serve cold.

BEEF TEA

Soak three-quarters of a pound of small pieces of lean steak in a pint of cold rainwater for half an hour, squeezing the beef occasionally; then put it on the fire. Cover and boil it slowly for ten minutes, removing the scum. Season with salt and serve hot.

OATMEAL GRUEL

Combine one quart boiling water, one tablespoon raw oatmeal, one-half teaspoonful salt. Place the water in a frying pan. Add the oatmeal and cook for two hours over a slow heat. Season with salt. Fill a cup ⅔ full with the hot gruel and fill the balance with cream or milk, stirring both together well.

MILK TOAST

Cut the bread in thin slices, paring off the crust and toast carefully until golden brown. Butter it lightly while hot. Have ready a teacupful of milk that has been slightly thickened with a teaspoonful of flour and salted to taste. Heat and pour over the toast and serve at once.

SOPS

Break up dried bread into a cup. Pour scalding water over, then drain off all excess water. Add sugar and cream to the bread and serve while warm. This is especially good for feeding babies.

BEAUTY REGIMENS

SOAP

1 can lye
10 c. melted fat or 5 c. lard &
  5 c. tallow

5 c. cold water
Borax (opt.)

Slowly add lye to cold water in earthenware. Do it outdoors or open the windows. Mixing lye and water produces heat. The solution will reach almost 200°. There will be strong fumes. You can see them and try not to breathe them because they will make you cough. Don't use anything but a wooden spoon, a long stick or paddle to stir with. Be careful not to splash it on your skin. Stir constantly until the lye dissolves. Let it cool to 70°-75°, if your fat is hog lard. If tallow, cool to 90°-95°. Heat melted fat to 80°-85°; 100°-110° for half lard and half tallow; 120°-130° for tallow. Large portion of fat gives a milder soap. Pour the fat slowly into the lye water when you have each at the right temperature. (Just go by the feel of the heat of the fat kettle, not too hot, not just warm.) Add Borax. Stir in one direction for 2 to 3 hours, sometimes 2½ hours. Soap starts out dark colored, getting lighter as you stir. It is ready to pour when it is like thick pea soup and drops trailed from the spoon or stick will stand momentarily on the surface. Pour into molds. Dip it out with a cup and pour.

LYE SOAP

6 lbs. cracklings, meat rinds,   **1 gal. water**
  fat scraps or old grease   **1 can lye**

Build fire under wash pot. Add ingredients. Keep fire high enough to allow ingredients to boil constantly, but not to boil over top of pot. Stir with wooden paddle. When lye has eaten up all visible cracklings, etc., put out fire and stir until soap is thick. It is very important you stir until cool enough that the lye will not settle. Takes about ½ day.

SHAMPOO FOR HAIR
(This Recipe Is Over 100 Years Old.)

Shave up to 3 tablespoons white soap, 3 teaspoonfuls powdered Borax, 3 teaspoons ammonia and 2 pints boiling water. Let it stand on the stove until all is dissolved. Use ½ to 1 cupful to a wash.

CHAPPED HANDS

1. Powdered starch is an excellent preventive of chapping of the hands when it is rubbed over them after washing. It will also prevent the needle in sewing from sticking and becoming rusty. It is advisable to have a small box of it in the workbox or basket and near your washbasin.

2. Equal parts of lemon juice, camphor and glycerine makes a splendid wash for chapped hands.

Hand Lotion

1. 1 cup glycerin, 1 cup bay rum, 2 cups rose water, ½ ounce tincture of benzoin, 1 large tablespoon quince seed. Mix all in order given.

2. An excellent preparation for the hands: 5 cents worth quince seed, simmer in one pint of water; strain and add equal quantity of pure glycerine and small portion of rose water. Shake well.

Wash For A Blotched Face

Rose water, three ounces; sulphate of zinc, one drachm; mix. Wet the face with it, gently dry it and then touch it over with cold cream, which also gently dry off.

To Remove Warts

The best application is said to be that of mono-hydrated nitric acid. The ordinary acid should not be used, because its caustic effects extend much farther than the points touched, while the action of the stronger acid here recommended is limited to the parts to which it is actually applied. Nitrate of silver is also frequently used with results and of late, a concentrated solution of chloral has been spoken of as efficient in destroying warts.

FRECKLES

1. Mix together buttermilk and lemon juice. Put on freckles to remove them.

2. Put sap from a grapevine on them.

3. Make a poultice of eggs, cream and epsom salts and spread on the freckles. Take off after it dries.

TO CLEAR A TANNED SKIN

Wash with a solution of carbonate of soda and a little lemon juice, then with the juice of unripe grapes.

CORNS ON FEET

Bread crumbs   **Cider vinegar**

Add enough fine bread crumbs to $\frac{1}{4}$ cup of cider vinegar to make a good poultice. Allow to stand for about $\frac{1}{2}$ hour, then apply this poultice upon retiring at night. In the morning the soreness will be gone, and the corn can be picked out. For a very obstinate corn, two or more applications may be required to effect a cure.

HOUSEHOLD TIPS

SHOE POLISH

To restore the color of black kid boots, take a small quantity of black ink, mix it with the white of an egg and apply with a soft sponge.

TO CLEAN SILVER

Table silver should be cleaned at least once or twice a week and can easily be kept in good order and polished brightly in this way: Have your dish pan half full of boiling water. Place your silver in so that it may become warm, then with a soft cloth dipped into the hot water, soaped and sprinkled with powdered borax, scour the silver well. Then rinse in clean hot water and dry with a clean, dry cloth.

HOMEMADE FURNITURE POLISH

1 oz. boiled linseed oil   1 oz. vinegar
1 oz. turpentine

Mix together. Use with soft cloth.

174

HERBAL SACHET

10 bay leaves, crumbled
2 T. dried sage
2 T. dried oregano
2 T. dried basil

2 T. dried thyme
2 dried lavender
3 T. dried rosemary
¼ c. arris root

Combine all ingredients in a medium bowl, then place 3 tablespoons of mixture on a 4 x 4-inch piece of cheesecloth. Tie corners together with a ribbon.

HINTS ON WASHING

Clothes should not be soaked overnight; it gives them a grey look and the soiled parts lying against the clean portions streak them. Rub the clothes in warm, not hot, water, for hot water sets, in place of removing the dirt. Wash flannels in lukewarm water and avoid rubbing soap upon flannels.

WASHING FLUID

Dissolve one can Babbit's lye in one gallon rain water. Let cool and add 10 cents worth of salts of tartar and 10 cents worth of ammonia. Use in washing and boiling water, a half teacupful to one-half boiler of water.

Solution For Taking Out Stains

1. Half pound chloride of lime, one and a half pounds salt soda; put both in a jar and pour one gallon of boiling water over. Stir until dissolved, then strain and bottle. Wet the stain with the solution and lay in the sun.

2. To take out tough stains from white clothes, use smashed apricot pits.

Remove Soot Stains

Perhaps it is not generally known that a cloth saturated with kerosene will speedily remove soot stains from the tea kettle or other tin utensils.

Cleaning Porcelain

To clean the brown from a porcelain kettle, boil peeled potatoes in it. The porcelain will be rendered nearly as white as when new.

Destroy Bad Smells

To remove the smell of onions an other odors from utensils, put some wood ashes into the vessel. Add boiling water and let it stand a short time on the back of the stove. A little vinegar boiling in a vessel on the stove while onions are cooking will destroy much of the onion odor.

To Clean Water Bottles

Put about two tablespoonfuls vinegar to one of salt and shake round for a few minutes. Then rinse with clear water.

Cures For household Pests

Rats are said to have such a dislike for potash, that if it is powdered and scattered around their haunts, they will leave them. A piece of rag well soaked in a solution of cayenne is a capital thing to put into rat and mice holes as they will not attempt to eat it. A plug of wood, covered with a piece of flannel, may be used to fill up their holes. Cockroaches and ants have a similar dislike of cayenne. A little strewed about a cellar will keep it clear of them.

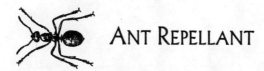 Ant Repellant

Oil of sassafras dropped on shelves will drive away ants.

Fly Repellant

Branches of the elder bush hung in the dining room will clear it of flies. It has an odor which the insects detest.

GLASS CLEANER

Two or three tablespoons of coal oil in a half bucket of lukewarm water is good for cleaning window glass.

REMOVE INK

Sapolio will remove ink stains from china and the hand.

INDEX OF RECIPES

COOKING ON THE TRAIL

UTOPIA - END OF THE TRAIL

BREADS

SIDE DISHES

MAIN DISHES

DESSERTS

THIS & THAT

NEW RECIPES FROM OLD FAVORITES

PIONEER HOME REMEDIES

MEDICINAL REMEDIES

FOOD FOR INVALIDS

BEAUTY REGIMENS

THE MORMON TRAIL COOKBOOK
MAKES THE PERFECT GIFT

The Mormon Trail Cookbook is the perfect gift for cooks, history buffs and cookbook collectors. If you would like to order additional copies, please return an order form with your check or money order to:

The Mormon Trail Cookbook
Morris Publishing
P.O. Box 233
Kearney, NE 68848

Please mail me ___ copies of *The Mormon Trail Cookbook* at $10.95 per copy and $2.00 for shipping and handling for each book.* I have enclosed my check/money order (made payable to Morris Publishing) in the amount of $_____ .
Mail my books to: (please type or print clearly)

Name _____

Address _____

City _____ State _____ Zip _____

*NE residents add 5% state sales tax and any local tax to your total order.

Please mail me___ copies of *The Mormon Trail Cookbook* at $10.95 per copy and $2.00 for shipping and handling for each book.* I have enclosed my check/money order (made payable to Morris Publishing) in the amount of $_____ .
Mail my books to: (please type or print clearly)

Name _____

Address _____

City _____ State _____ Zip _____

*NE residents add 5% state sales tax and any local tax to your total order.

Please mail me ___ copies of *The Mormon Trail Cookbook* at $10.95 per copy and $2.00 for shipping and handling for each book.* I have enclosed my check/money order (made payable to Morris Publishing) in the amount of $_____ .
Mail my books to: (please type or print clearly)

Name _____

Address _____

City _____ State _____ Zip _____

*NE residents add 5% state sales tax and any local tax to your total order.

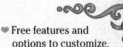
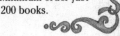

Create your own cookbook
with Cookbooks by Morris Press

Call for Free Information (no obligation)

1-800-445-6621 ext. CB

Or complete and send the Business Reply Card
below. See other side for details.